# Praise for
# A Mirthful Spirit

*The chemistry in this book is great, providing fun, healthful "inner-tainment" that can add days to your life and life to your days.*

—Dale Anderson, M.D. author of
*Act Now* and *Never Act Your Age*

*A Mirthful Spirit provides a recipe for life "ever-laughing." It is a fresh approach to using laughter to live life to the fullest.*

—Annie Glasgow, author of
*Gift to the Present: Wellderly Wisdom*

# A
# Mirthful
# Spirit

May the music &
laughter warm
your heart + bell
your spirit for
living well
Mirthfully,
Mary Huntley

Wishing
you a
joyous
life.
Edna Thayer

# A Mirthful Spirit

## Embracing Laughter for Wellness

### Mary Huntley & Edna Thayer

Beaver's Pond Press, Inc.
Edina, Minnesota

ISBN-13: 978-1-59298-165-6
ISBN-10: 1-59298-165-8

Library of Congress Catalog Number: 2006909419

Printed in the United States of America

First Printing: January 2007
Second Printing: January 2008

11  10  09  08     5  4  3  2

Beaver's Pond Press, Inc.

7104 Ohms Lane, Suite 101
Edina, MN  55439
(952) 829-8818
www.BeaversPondPress.com

To order, visit www.BookHouseFulfillment.com
or call 1-800-901-3480. Reseller discounts available.

For more information please visit: **www.mirthfulspirit.com**

# Dedication

This book is mirthfully dedicated to our husbands
Kennes C. Huntley and David L. Thayer
and to our
respective families of adult children and grandchildren,
the people with whom we love laughing the most
and who nurture our mirthful spirits.

## Mary Huntley's Family

Kendy and Brian Bibbs, Griffin and Samantha,
Cal and Tami Huntley, Taylor and Cade

## Edna Thayer's Family

Scott and Ginger Thayer, Ashley and Yan Clermont, Will Thayer and
Whitney Werner, Molly and Hannah Thayer,
Tammy and Dan Appel, Patrick, Kelly, Nathan, Matthew and
Andrea Appel, Allison and Andrew Cooney,
Brenda and Keith Eisenschenk, Mathew and Rachel

# Contents

# Acknowledgements

With grateful hearts and mirthful spirits the authors wish to acknowledge the contributions of family, laughter enthusiasts, book development experts, and friends who have shared the journey of creating this book in a variety of ways.

- The spouses and families of Mary and Edna were always there and understood the commitment to creating a manuscript. Ken Huntley and Dave Thayer helped in many ways to support, encourage, critique, and provide mirthful lightheartedness at the right moments.

- Our research participants shared their experiences which led to the framework and taught us important and valuable reflections, wisdom, and perspectives. We thank Sandra Schuette for her scholarly partnership and dialogue with us in the 2004 research project.

- We are abundantly grateful to Dr. Kaye Herth for reading our early beginnings, writing the foreword, as well as offering prompt counsel, encouragement, and welcomed support.

- Dr. Dale Anderson gave inspiration to Edna as she launched her career in humor. We thank him and his partner, Annie Glasgow for writing endorsements for the book and acknowledging their unending commitment to laughter for healing and wellness. Dr. Joel Goodman was an unknowing inspiration to Mary as she launched her scholarly pursuit. We express our appreciation for giving permission to use some of his humorous sayings, for providing an endorsement, and for embracing every opportunity to assure that laughter matters.

# Acknowledgements

- Delta Kappa Gamma Society International awarded a Golden Gift Special Projects stipend to be used toward the completion of this book. We gratefully extend our gratitude for their generous gift and confidence in us that we could accomplish the goal.

- The Cindy Scherb Research Dissemination Award was presented to us by Mu Lambda Chapter of Sigma Theta Tau International. We are very thankful to receive this financial assistance to share our message that laughter makes a difference in the personal and professional lives of everyone.

- We believed the inspirational poem, "Children Learn What They Live," needed to be in the book. Dr. Dorothy Law Nolte, her family, and publisher are to be commended for providing ways to continue sharing her work.

- Beaver's Pond Press, most specifically Milton Adams and staff members Kellie Hultgren and Judith Palmateer, are the best. We express our pleasure in working with them and thank them for their coaching and abundant support as they linked us with such experts as, Dr. Kurt Burch with his editing skills and creative suggestions for change and Tom Heller and Jay Monroe of Mori Studio for their book design expertise.

- Leah Hesla, Mary's niece and musicologist from Austin, Texas, provided expertise, support, and encouragement for musing about the synergism of laughter and music. Mary's life-long friend, Elizabeth Nelson Shriver, from Cleveland Heights, Ohio, a seasoned library specialist; and Allison Cooney, Edna's granddaughter, and college student in St. Peter, Minnesota gave fresh eyes in sharing their honest reflections and perspectives as manuscript reviewers.

- We appreciate the school leaders who shared outcomes and expectations for promoting healthy school environments where learning, respect, and responsibility thrive.

- Many people have visited with us along this journey, encouraged us to keep going, and shared their stories of laughter and wellness. Their inspiration and insights have provided immeasurable moments of mirthfulness, chuckles, and joy.

# Foreword

*A mirthful spirit provides a bridge through difficult times
that can lead to relaxation, hope,
connectedness, perspective and joy,
and can engender a sense of overall wellness.*

—Kaye A. Herth

A mirthful spirit lies at the very heart of human wellbeing. This book traces historical understandings of the social roles of laughter, including the recent recognition of a mirthful spirit as a resource for individual and group wellness. Both authors of this book are highly respected learners and scholars of mirth and laughter. Within these pages the authors capture and convey the value of mirth in humor development and wellness.

This book is full of many wonderful stories to illustrate and embrace mirth and laughter as sources of wellbeing. Individuals of all ages and walks of life will benefit. The authors carefully weave their own scholarly work with a comprehensive overview of research by others in the "mirth field." Excellent resources and suggestions pepper the chapters and appear in the appendices. Although this book is based on theory and research, it comes to life for the reader by presenting in simple and straightforward language specific ways to kindle and engender the mirthful spirit in oneself and in one's home, work, and school environments. Mirth is a formidable power for helping people cope with and grow from the challenges in everyday life and to embrace laughter for wellness.

Since people must become receptive to mirth and laughter, the best humor must be appropriate, timely, and tasteful. The authors help readers distinguish positive and negative humor and to use humor in healthy and happy ways.

The growing body of research on humor and laughter is compelling, but people must now incorporate the lessons and insights into their lives. As the authors note in Chapter One: "The true measure that positive laughter makes a difference will be realized when we begin to tell ourselves, our health-care providers, and others that intentionally laughing every day facilitates our recuperation or our wellness."

The authors warmly and engagingly help us see that we can learn and nurture a mirthful spirit. Yet simply reading the book is not enough; the book beckons us to put its lessons into action and to turn this knowledge into tools for enhancing our wellness and happiness.

*Kaye A. Herth, Ph.D. and Registered Nurse (R.N.)*
*Fellow in the American Academy of Nursing*
*Dean, College of Allied Health and Nursing*
*Minnesota State University, Mankato*
*Mankato, Minnesota*

# PART I

## Embracing Mirth and Laughter for Wellness

# 1

# Sharing Mirth and Laughter

*Mirthfulness shared is double the mirth.*
—Mary Huntley and Edna Thayer

Embracing and nurturing mirth, lightness, and levity in your life will lead you to laugh more. Recognizing and using mirth and laughter will actually improve your health and wellness. This book addresses humor, mirth, laughter, and wellness. We want you to smile and laugh your way to health, vigor, and wellness. Laugh often—what a simple prescription!

We learned this, in part, from the many people we have studied and interviewed. Here's what they tell us.

> *Laughter is God's hand on a troubled world.... Laughter makes me feel good inside.... One can even think better.*

> *Laughter is spontaneous...an expression of joy...relief or antidote to the tough times.*

> *Laughter keeps you going...is a sense of relief...can help overcome depression...a healthy body function.*

> *I think anyone is better because of laughter. Laughter solidifies a group...is contagious. Laughter with others is bonding.*

*Laughter is a gift from God...an outward expression of inner happiness...has a spiritual quality...brings out the inner spirit.*

*Laughter is the music of the soul...makes you feel better...is very healing.*

*Laughter is the sound of being happy.... Laughter is the most important thing I do...takes away my fears.*

*Laughter...is inner joy...gives me joy in living...is sharing joy and moments of fellowship and friendship.*

Opportunities for mirth and laughter abound. Mirth is a feeling of joy or delight, the emotional response to humor. Laughter is the physical response to humor. To experience mirth, joy, and delight requires being and becoming receptive to humor. That is, the world becomes funnier and more amusing as we become more receptive to joy and humor. And as we become more receptive, we become healthier. The sources of humor and joy in our lives differ depending upon culture, circumstance, and individual taste, but the basic relationship, according to Bessie Anderson Stanley is crystal clear: "Laugh often, love much, and live well."

This book will not help you tell better jokes or become funnier. Rather, we discuss how to become more receptive to humor. That is, we focus on receiving humor, not on broadcasting amusingly. We want to help you adjust your "humor antennae" so you can receive more humorous messages and create a warm environment. We want you to intentionally incorporate laughter and mirth into your personal and professional lives. If you do, you'll promote your health and wellness.

What do we mean? To enjoy good *health* is to enjoy a sound mind and body. We think that *wellness* is a broader term. Indeed, one may be struggling with an illness or be actually unhealthy, yet experience wellness.

Even while coping with adversity, laughter fosters harmony by providing perspective, by helping us bond with each other, by improving our attitude and outlook, and by directly creating physical, psychological, emotional, spiritual, and social wellbeing. Laughter is light and festive. It is also serious business. The serious business is your health, wellness, and satisfaction with life. So, with your lighthearted lens in focus, let's get serious about humor, mirth, and laughter.

> *Prepare for mirth, for mirth becomes a feast.*
> —William Shakespeare

We've been serious about humor, mirth, and laughter for years. Here is our story of how we came to share the whole gamut of mirthfulness and laughter.

Mary Huntley earned a nursing degree in 1962 and two graduate degrees in nursing in subsequent years. Mary has amassed over 30 years of experience in nursing education, primarily at Minnesota State University (MSU), Mankato. Her interest in humor and wellness was sparked in 1984 by her daughter's research for a high school essay. When Mary enrolled in a doctoral program to earn her Ph.D., she conducted research on the connections between laughter and wellness. She has studied laughter and wellness extensively, and much of her research lies at the heart of this book.

Edna Thayer, the Laughing Lady, is founder of "Humor THAYER-apy." She is a registered nurse and has earned two Master's degrees. During her 40 years of experience in the nursing field, leadership and management were consistent parts of her career. She developed seminars for staff on "Stress Relief through Humor" as part of one of her leadership positions. The success of the seminars led to hundreds of talks presented to people from all walks of life.

We were colleagues for a number of years as nurse educators and maintained our professional connections when Edna accepted leadership positions in hospitals. Later we teamed with another work associate, Linda Beer, to write a history of the first 50 years of the School of Nursing at MSU, published in 2003, *Celebrating the First Fifty Years: An Interpretive Essay.*

Our passion for nursing gave us energy for the first book project. Our passion for humor, laughter, and wellness gave us enthusiasm for writing this book. As nurse educators we loved teaching and soon learned it requires a great sense of humor. Working with others in education and administration requires an even greater sense of humor and an ability to laugh at ourselves and with others. Both believe the role of administrator requires substantial doses of laughter, prayer, and vitamin C to stay healthy and energized.

We realized one day in our retirement years as we worked on telling the story of the MSU School of Nursing's first 50 years that it would be fun to tell our story of humor, laughter, and wellness. Both of us had been telling others about the value of laughter through courses and seminars. Mary focused on research, hoping to describe the relationship between laughter and wellness, then teach others about it. Edna generated abundant laughter with her presentations on the topic. We decided to join the scholarship of laughter and wellness together with the practice of laughing to relieve stress. Our book combines research, years of study, and broad experiences to deliver an important message: Laughter can improve and sustain your health and wellness.

From working together on this book, we discovered three major understandings—three "aha's." One "aha" is that people not associated with health care, describe wellness as "purposeful living," as having an "attitude of acceptance" understood as "enjoyable unity." Such people do not describe wellness as only absence of disease. Rather, they have a much deeper understanding.

A second "aha" was the tremendous need to passionately tell others to be intentional about laughing–only then will it make a difference in promoting wellness. There are huge numbers of resources available in the literature and on the Internet that proclaim the strong connections among laughter-health-wellness. We have selected a few. We came to realize from our work together that everything in life, besides breathing, requires people to be intentional. One must be intentional about going to sleep, eating, exercising, playing, socializing, taking care of health-care appointments, saving money, being safe, parenting, working, and becoming spiritual, to name a few.

Thus, we weave an important plea throughout the book: Be intentional about laughter. Some scholars want more evidence to document the relationship. We say why wait. Smile. Giggle. Chuckle. Guffaw. Create your own evidence. Laugh positively and intentionally. Then tell others how good you feel.

The third "aha" came from our research-study participants. They consistently report the pain and harm they felt and feel—often decades later—

from being teased and taunted. The lesson is clear: Teasing, taunting, and laughing AT others is harmful. Don't do it. Maybe if we all work to stop teasing we can also help stop the taunting, bullying, and violence that may follow. We strongly emphasize this point.

Our purpose is to share our passion and our collective experience in examining this wonderful phenomenon of mirth and laughter. However, this is not a joke book. Not all forms of humor are funny to everyone. Enjoying a mirthful spirit and embracing it for laughter is much more than jokes and funny stories. We trust that what we share is acceptable since our intention is to offend no one.

Human beings are extremely fortunate to have a built-in, ready-to-be-used mechanism that costs nothing and can create tremendous value. We hope our readers will accept the compelling evidence about mirth and laughter as a healthful tonic and will embrace these insights to promote and maintain their own wellness. Being intentional about nurturing one's mirthful spirit may sound too easy. For some it *is* easy. For others it requires conscious thinking and action. Practice. Try it. Do it. Purposefully taking advantage of opportunities to focus on what makes one feel mirthful, as well as to laugh AT ONESELF and WITH OTHERS leads to enjoyable unity.

The book is organized into four parts. Part I unveils the laughter-wellness connection. The message here is acknowledge what makes you laugh, embrace it regularly, and it will help you be well. The physical benefits of laughter for vitality are many. Ways in which laughter leads to social bonding and increased sociability are very compelling. Altogether we make the case for an intentional perspective of mirth and laughter for wellness.

Part II tells how to nurture your mirthful spirit, your laughter. Nurturing laughter for yourself has numerous advantages. Even when feeling distressed, tense, or ill, mirthfulness and even a little bit of laughter can be helpful. Information about the harmful use of laughter is described fully, since misuse of teasing in our society happens all too frequently. Humor and laughter have a developmental process. We offer tips for nurturing their growth positively.

Part III focuses on laughter for the work place. While being sensitive to the job at hand, supporting fun at work and caring about others is good for any business. Information abounds in this section for creating successful use of humor in all kinds of work places. Since our backgrounds include health care and education, more specific ideas are provided for workers in these fields.

Part IV describes the serious side of laughter. There is a tremendous amount of information about laughter that is very serious, even though when we first think about laughter, we may naturally think about being silly and funny. Laughter is shared from the perspectives of history, culture, religion, music, theory, and research.

The wisdom shared with us by our research participants is sprinkled throughout the book. We include some of their wisdom, the wisdom of other experts, as well as our own ponderings with you in such forms as quotes, acronyms, epigrams, and poetic musings.

Numerous resources are listed in the Appendices. Some provide humor, mirth, and laughter we have enjoyed. We include a variety of publications. Those cited in the book are listed in the Bibliography, whereas some others we have read or reviewed, but not cited in the book, are listed as References.

We would be delighted if you as a reader of the book were to pay attention to the ways in which mirthfulness and laughter really contribute to making your life better. The true measure that positive laughter makes a difference will be realized when we begin to tell ourselves, our health-care providers, and others that intentionally laughing every day facilitates our recuperation or our wellness.

*Positive laughter matters and is the celebration of a loving heart for living well.*

—Mary Huntley and Edna Thayer

# 2
# Laughing for Wellness

*At the height of laughter the universe is flung into a kaleidoscope of new possibilities.*

—Jean Huston

Laughter is the happiest sound humans hear. Stories abound about how humor and laughter have helped people survive horrific situations. If humor and laughter can help in those situations, think of the less severe and less complicated situations in which people could call upon their mirthful spirits to heal, improve health, and foster wellness.

People often cite nutrition, exercise, rest, self-esteem, positive relationships, education, and a belief in a higher power as essential ingredients for health and wellness. Humor, a mirthful spirit, and laughter are not regularly mentioned, but we think they should be.

This chapter shares views of selected authorities on health and wellness and shares stories from specific people about the influence of laughter on wellness. We want you to feel empowered by laughter and about laughter. Feel empowered and healthy. Feel the mirthful spirit! Take advantage of laughter to improve your health and outlook. By becoming receptive to humor and attentive to mirth, you embrace laughter for wellness.

*Seven days without laughter makes one weak.*

—Joel Goodman

# Reflecting On Cautions And Celebrations About Laughing For Wellness

*Humor* [laughter] *is a wonderful way to prevent a hardening of the attitudes.*

—Joel Goodman

Reading the book by James Walsh, M.D., on *Laughter and Health*, published nearly eight decades ago, causes one to pause, reflect, and wonder why it has taken people so long to accept the truths about laughter and health and to make a conscious effort to give laughter an intentional place in one's life. An Irishman once said, "Life is a dangerous thing…very few of us get out alive." Some interpret this as a good reason to live each day as well as possible, accept what comes along, cope with it, and let laughter keep life in perspective.

Dr. Robert Provine, author of *Laughter: A Scientific Investigation* (2000), reports on several studies that examine connections between laughter and health. Due to faulty research designs, human conditions, and other limitations, Provine resists the temptation to support the laughter and health connection, and, because of the difficulties of conducting controlled laboratory studies, he warns that fewer studies may be conducted in the future. Nonetheless, he and many others advocate indulging in laughter for health benefits. It cannot hurt!

Rod Martin, a longtime investigator of health and laughter, reported in 2002 that more methodologically rigorous studies were needed before he could definitively conclude that laughter improves immunity, pain tolerance, blood pressure, longevity, or illness symptoms. In 2004 Martin published his view that people with a higher sense of humor are more satisfied with their health.

Many writers on the subjects of laughter, health, and wellness draw on anecdotal reports from individuals. Humor audio and video tapes, CDs, "Joke of the Day" telephone lines, Internet humor, and favorite comic books and cartoons have been identified consistently as helpful resources by those recuperating over a long period of time.

Our own research participants shared the following anecdotal stories of how humor, a mirthful spirit, and laughter helped them. In order to protect their identities, different names are used in the stories.

Earl suffered from painful shingles for many years and needed a consistent regimen of pain medication. He willingly attempted every treatment that was suggested to him to relieve the pain. Nothing really worked. He learned to accept his condition by being positive and not buying into the mournful way people would respond to him. He said, "You have to put on a good face, perhaps lead any hilarity that you feel might help the situation, which in turn then aids me indirectly."

Beth described her unhappy childhood years. Her parents were unhappy, laughter was seldom heard in the home, and there were many difficulties. She felt afraid to laugh and to cry. Her feelings were squelched. There was no freedom to feel silly, to lighten up, and to just be loose. During her adult years she, her mother, and sister had opportunities to travel together and to get to know each other better. They found themselves laughing freely while visiting galleries or while doing some other tourist activities. Beth and her sister made a pact to never lose their ability to lighten up and to laugh.

Nancy decided after her heart attack that she could not let herself become lonely. She would call someone to talk. They would get their laughter going and get into a good feeling. "During my recovery from my heart attack I found that laughter takes away my fears. I found I could talk myself into angina pain and it was just as easy to relieve it with laughter. Laughter is the best way plus being around other people."

Riley talked about being in the hospital frequently during his adult life. He said that in recovery the best things that happened to him were when people came to visit him and made him laugh.

In his younger years Tom said, "I was a physical wreck, headaches for 40 years, took 6-15 aspirins each day for 20 years, smoked for 30 years. I didn't understand depression until it happened to me. When I lost my wife in later years, it put a crimp in my laughter for quite awhile. With medication and laughter I have been able to overcome it. I go to lots of things and enjoy them. I have humor to read in the bathroom. I think one of the nicest things you can say about somebody is he/she is funny. When not concerned about your body—that is wellness."

Marie said that reading the comic strips in the daily newspaper was a good way to begin her day. "It sets the tone for the day," and gives her a positive outlook.

Sarah talked about the loss of her young child. She was very sad and felt as though she would never laugh again. Years later, through the encouragement of a friend, she agreed to help out in an elementary school as a volunteer. She found that the smiles, enthusiasm, mirthfulness, and laughter from children and teachers provided the resources she needed to heal. She was soon able to return to teaching on a full-time basis and her ability to laugh returned as well.

Even if people do not believe laughter is the best medicine, it is a good medicine. The spark to begin the laughter is unimportant. Whether you laugh at a good joke or mirthfully smile from pure delight makes no difference.

Annette Goodheart, Ph.D., is a popular presenter on the subject of laughter. She educates and entertains many people in the health and helping professions and people from all walks of life across the United States. Dr. Goodheart lectures and writes about *Laughter Therapy.* Her lessons about the value of laughter are used for therapy, therapy most do not realize they need.

She offers uncomplicated lessons on the complex emotions of fear, anger, and boredom. When any of these emotions appears in response to a situation, it is healthy to express the emotion. If the emotions are kept bottled inside the person, they come out in other ways such as through physical or emotional illness. In addition, if the emotion is not expressed when it is first acknowledged, then it can grow into something bigger and more serious. For example, fear can move into emotions of worry, tension, or even aggressive behavior. If angry feelings are not dealt with, then the anger may appear as sarcasm, hostile behavior, or even hate. Being hopeless, helpless, or apathetic might be the outcome of feelings of boredom. One way to prevent this is to express the emotion and learn to use laughter as a way of releasing the tension associated with the emotion. Thus, the sounds of laughter may communicate the underlying emotional tension from fear, anger, or boredom. This is another reason for not squelching laughter even though it may sound unusual. It may be serving the person in a very useful way. Goodheart's first recommendation in a list of 25 ways to help oneself laugh is to "fake it until you make it." Force the laughter until you can express it easily and naturally.

Annette Goodheart also strongly advocates the notion of "Tee Hee." In fact it became so important that it is the first chapter in her book *Laughter Therapy.* She believed that anything painful, serious, or stressful can become less so by using the "Tee Hee" approach. The idea is to say aloud what is causing one to feel pain, tension, or anger, then end the statement with "Tee Hee." Soon the "Tee Hee" words create a laughable moment and then more laughter occurs. It sounds simple and it may be, if one is open to making it work. Even then it may take several repetitions of saying it to make the "Tee Hee" really work. Goodheart is not advocating laughing AT anything. Rather, laugh WITH something in hopes of creating a more playful attitude toward something quite stressful. Saying the stressor and "Tee Hee" phrase over and over releases tension and allows laughter to do its work for the person. This concept can be used with anything—from an aggravating object such as a lawn mower that won't start to coping with a serious diagnosis of cancer.

Bernie Siegel, M.D., is a well-known, well-published physician who uses humor and laughter as a regular part of his medical practice. Laughter is part of the medical care Dr. Siegel gives. He claims, "You can't stay afraid when you are laughing." The laughing times create hope and foster wonderful memories for the family. For dying patients, their end of life becomes joyful and filled with love because of family togetherness and the ability of the family to laugh together until the end.

Health-care providers working with cancer patients report they believe humor and laughter enhance wellness. Therapeutic humor promotes health and wellness by uplifting the mind, body, and spirit of patients and family members coping with illness. One form of cancer care uses a model for quality of life. Indeed, humor and laughter may enhance all four dimensions of cancer care: physical, psychological, social, and spiritual. The recommendation is to begin interventions with the gentlest kind of humor, which is pleasant smiling or mirthfulness.

The healthy use of mirth must be surrounded with understanding, support, and love. One can have good intentions for sharing humor with another person. However, if that person is unable to sense the mirth or be receptive to it, then the mirth is unable to work. Once again, the connection between laughter and health and wellness is not automatic.

*Laughter is free, legal, has no calories, no cholesterol, no preservatives, no artificial ingredients, and is absolutely safe.*
—Dale Irvin

## Defining Health And Wellness

*Never go to a doctor whose office plants have died.*
—Erma Bombeck

Many people think health and wellness are the same. We think they are different.

According to the dictionary, "health" is derived from the words "hale" and "whole," which mean free from disease or infirmity and referring to soundness and vigor. Yet most health-care professionals and people in general regard health as more than freedom from disease and illness. Health encompasses mind, body, and spirit.

Andrew Weil, M.D., internationally known for his depth and breadth of knowledge of healing, writes in his 1995 book on *Health and Healing* that health is much more than absence of disease or illness. He states that "health is a dynamic and harmonious equilibrium of all the elements and forces making up and surrounding a human being." He further states in his book and later in a 2005 issue of *Time* magazine that health is related to wholeness and wholeness is related to balance. He does not explicitly refer to humor and laughter affecting health. From his perspective there are many things that contribute to health and happiness at any stage of life. We believe humor, mirth, and laughter are key contributors.

Ryan and Travis, in their 1991 book on *Wellness*, state that some also regard wellness as attention to fitness, nutrition, supplements, and selected complementary therapies. However, from their perspective wellness is much more. "Wellness is the bridge that takes people into realms far beyond treatment or therapy and into the domain of self-responsibility and self-empowerment." Humor and play are part of the equation that promotes wellness.

*The best doctors in the world are Dr. Diet, Dr. Quiet,*
*and Dr. Merryman.*

—Jonathan Swift

Carolyn Chambers Clark, in her book *Wellness Nursing: Concepts, Theory, Research, and Practice* (1986), defined wellness as:

> *a process of moving toward greater awareness of oneself and the environment leading toward ever-increasing planned interactions with the dimensions of nutrition, fitness, stress, environment, interpersonal relationships, and self-care responsibility.*

By this definition, a person assumes responsibility for wellness, and such wellness is a step beyond health. People can be coping with different stages of illness and still perceive themselves as well. More often than not, people are experiencing wellness as a process that is dynamic, always changing. Even though people are working to promote various aspects of their health, they may describe themselves as being in a state of wellness or moving toward wellness.

More recently, Clark (2000 and 2002) states that a focus on wellness brings people into active participation to find a balance that is right for each person, physically, socially, emotionally, and spiritually. People are generally experts in evaluating their own wellness. Achieving awareness, deriving satisfaction, and seeking balance become the important wellness goals.

Both Nola Pender (1996) and Clark remind us of an even broader look at wellness. Wellness can be viewed from the perspective of one person, a family, a community, as well as the environment or even the society. Even though we may address laughter more at the individual level, we support the use of laughter to spark the quest for greater wellness at each of these levels.

All of these health and wellness experts are in sync with *Healthy People 2010*, objectives directed by the U. S. Department of Health and Human Services. Public health workers and health care providers are working together in a plan for those living in America to engage in healthy behaviors and to prevent or reduce disease. The www.healthypeople.gov website explains the initiative. Even comedian Bill Cosby is part of the plan. He joined the Surgeon General in launching the health goals for 2010 with public service announcements. What an insightful connection—Cosby, symbolizing laughter, and the Surgeon General addressing wellness.

Some people in life are basically grumpy, grouchy, crabby, and pessimistic. We all know people like this. They tend to see their cups as half-empty, rather than half-full. Others become pessimistic when their health changes for the worse. With such a view of life, it is difficult for them to be open to humor and to use laughter to change a negative perspective on their lives.

People at any stage of life may be coping with significant health issues. Their health or healthfulness is determined by their attention to treatments that may help them to live with the problem. Managing health issues successfully also promotes wellness. If one believes that attending church or including prayer in one's life is essential for health and wellness, then doing so requires intentional action. Similarly, including laughter in one's life also leads to wellness and needs to be intentional. Everything a person does intentionally to assure being as healthy as possible, along with nurturing of a mirthful spirit, leads to wellness.

*...the greater part of our happiness or misery depends on our dispositions and not on our circumstances.*

—Martha Washington

# Wellness As Enjoyable Unity

*The longest distance in the world is the 12 inches from the head to the heart, and laughter is the vehicle to get you there.*

—Linda J. Allen

We define wellness as *enjoyable unity*. We had help with this definition. The 42 research participants in our studies defined wellness in their own words. Their definitions share this notion of enjoyable unity. Men and women in the 1988 and 2004 research studies consistently referred to a person as an integrated being of mind, body, and spirit. When one aspect of a person is not in harmony or is out of balance, then that aspect affects all of the other parts. Thus, a person functions as a unit. A person is whole or harmonious when his or her physical, psychological, emotional, spiritual, and social features complement and balance each other. *Unity* refers to the balance of mind, body, and spirit. *Enjoyable* means that people find pleasure in daily living and in choosing what they want and can do. Here are some of our research participants' definitions.

> *Wellness is a chosen, balanced state of mind, body, and spirit in which the person is able to cope with adverse stimuli, is able to experience feelings of security and contentment, and expresses a positive and hopeful attitude about life.*

> *Wellness is an attitude of acceptance, harmony, and freedom to enjoy being and doing what one can do.*

> *Wellness is a personal sense of wholeness, being at peace with who you are, and functioning in the world pleasantly, meaningfully, and purposefully.*

# What Connects Laughter And Wellness?:
## Purposeful Living And Attitude Of Acceptance

*Laughter is an instant vacation.*

—Milton Berle

Research participants in our 2004 study described how laughter and wellness are connected. They told us what L-A-U-G-H-T-E-R is, as described in the acronym:

**L** *Life is more enjoyable when humor and mirth are present.*

**A** *A way to dump emotional garbage and live across it.*

**U** *Use as the pump primer for wellness as it makes you feel better.*

**G** *Good feelings result. Laughter makes you feel that life is worthwhile.*

**H** *Helps foster a change in perspective and makes you feel invigorated.*

**T** *Tension is relieved.*

**E** *Essential ingredient of and an expression of one's wellness.*

**R** *Relaxing, stimulates thinking, creates diversion, enhances productivity.*

They told us what W-E-L-L-N-E-S-S is:

**W** *Wholeness, a sense of personal wholeness.*

**E** *Enjoying life, the peace and freedom to enjoy.*

**L** *Learning to adapt to changes and accepting them.*

**L** *Living as doing what one can do.*

**N** *Nurturing a positive attitude.*

**E** *Emotional, psychological, physical, social, and spiritual harmony.*

**S** *Satisfaction and being at peace with who you are.*

**S** *Sense of functioning pleasantly, meaningfully, and purposefully.*

Laughter gives us a sense of purpose in living. Remarkable links between laughter and wellness include being productive, being able to think, feeling invigorated, and believing that life is worthwhile. Laughter is invaluable for purposeful living and wellness.

Even during times of emotional, physical, or spiritual pain, participants talked about how laughter was helpful in their lives. Being mirthful, smiling, and being open to pleasantness were aspects of laughter that entered their lives. This kind of laughter helped them to accept what was happening and to experience a sense of wellness.

These responses confirm what many experts and lay-people believe: Wellness is broader than health. Our research participants' views also coincide with anecdotal evidence about the connections between laughter and wellness.

To enjoy the numerous benefits of laughter, a person must be receptive to humor in the events and happenings of life. The person's reactions— from mirth to guffaws—promote physical vitality. Social bridging, which we call *sociability*, creates emotional and social nourishment, supportive fun, hopefulness, balance, purpose, and meaning to life. A sense of purposeful living and an attitude of acceptance not only link laughter to wellness, but also boost the connection. Again we emphasize the point: Being open and receptive to smiling and laughable moments creates good conditions for new or continued wellness.

*Genuine laughing is the vent of the soul, the nostrils of the heart, and it is just as necessary for health and happiness as spring water is for a trout.*

—Josh Billings

# Intentionally Laughing For Wellness

*We don't laugh because we are happy,*
*we are happy because we laugh.*

—William James

We are describing the power of laughter. Think about it. Laughter is a generous, miraculous gift we can readily and endlessly give to ourselves and to others. Make sure laughter becomes a meaningful, purposeful, and intentional part of your life. Have a laugh and see what happens. Most people say they felt a lot better after a good giggle or a hearty belly laugh. The road to wellness is shorter if you prevent illness in the first place. So take a short-cut: Intentionally laugh to pave your way to wellness. Enjoyable unity is only a few laughs away.

*Laughter need not be cut out of anything,*
*since it improves everything.*

—James Thurber

# 3
# Laughing for Vitality

*Laughter is the pump primer of life.*
—Research Participant

A mirthful spirit leads to laughter. Laughing leads to vitality and sociability, which both enhance wellness. Vitality is strength and vigor, the ability to live and be active. In our research study we use the word *vitality* to describe physiological benefits arising from a mirthful spirit and from laughter. We describe these benefits with the acronym V-I-T-A-L-I-T-Y.

**V** *Vitalizes life itself*

**I** *Initiates internal jogging*

**T** *Thwarts infections*

**A** *Alleviates pain*

**L** *Lightens stress*

**I** *Increases brain-cell functioning*

**T** *Tickles the funny bone*

**Y** *Yields healthful rewards*

## V  Vitalizes Life Itself

*A good hearty laugh makes us tingle with renewed vitality out to the very ends of our fingers and toes.*
—John Walsh, M.D.

Humor and a mirthful spirit create a vital spark that animates all humans. The notion that humor and laughter are good for one's health can be traced far back in history. References from the Bible are sprinkled throughout this book. Hippocrates wrote that physicians should cultivate a serious and respectable image while at the same time using wit in interacting with their patients. Voltaire, the famous French philosopher, wrote, "The art of medicine is amusing the patient while nature takes its course." As early as 1928, Dr. John Walsh wrote *Laughter and Health*, describing laughter as movements of the diaphragm which in turn massage all the organs above and below, thereby improving the circulation and function of these organs. He stated that laughter helps breathing, heart functioning, and digestion and makes one feel better all around. Walsh further stated that laughter also affects the mind by brushing away dread and fear which are the basis of many diseases. It fosters an endocrine balance which helps replace worry, anger, and fear with a cheerful attitude. More recently, Eggenberger and Huntley (1999) used the following definition of vitality in their report on envisioning health care: "Vitality is the capacity to grow and develop with mental and physical energy and enthusiasm for life."

## I  Initiates Internal Jogging

*When we laugh, muscles are activated. When we stop laughing, these muscles relax. . . . Many people with arthritis, rheumatism, and other painful conditions, benefit greatly from a healthy dose of laughter.*
—William Fry, M.D.

In 1986 William Fry, M.D., of Stanford Medical School, likened laughing to internal exercising. He published further reports in the 1990s.

He stated that all organs above and below the diaphragm are jogged. The heart rate and pulse increase and respirations are enhanced. It helps clear the lungs and airways, and oxygen exchange in the lungs is increased. The moving of the digestive organs even improves digestion. This is the arousal state. After the laughter ceases, normal relaxation occurs, and the heart rate and respirations return to normal. He said that ten seconds of vigorous laughing can double the heart rate as much as ten minutes of strenuous rowing. The best part is that one does not need a boat and water to laugh. This exercise can be done without any props. It is a great way to exercise for someone confined to a bed.

## T   Thwarts Infections

*Question: What do you get when you kiss a canary?*
*Answer: Chirpes.*
*It's a canarial disease but it's tweetable.*

—Shannon Lawrence, R.N.

Several studies suggest laughter enhances a body's immune system and thwarts or prevents infections. Laughter diminishes the stress hormones cortisol and epinephrine which in turn increases the body's natural ability to fight infections.

Studies by Dillon and Baker show that the level of immunoglobulin antibody (IgA) in the mouth's saliva increases with laughter. This helps the body prevent and fight diseases of the upper respiratory system by combating germs as they enter the mouth. Berk and McGhee find that laughter increases the amount of antibodies IgM and IgG, and the complement C3, all of which enhance the inflammation, chemotaxis, and lysis of target cells. Laughter increases levels of interferon gamma, which inhibits virus replication, promotes antigen processing, and activates macrophages. *This means that people who laugh a lot should have fewer colds, fewer tumors, and less cancer.*

Natural killer activity (NKA) cells are lymphocytes whose purpose is to destroy tumor cells. Laughter increases the number of NKA cells as well as B and T cells which are essential to the immune response.

Relationships between our emotional experience and the immune response are studied in a rapidly expanding field of knowledge called psychoneuroimmunology. *This field of study supports the view that the immune system is suppressed by anxiety, depression, and negativity and enhanced by positive emotions such as joy, hope, faith, love, purpose, and determination.*

## A  Alleviates Pain

*Mirth is God's medicine.*

—Henry Ward Beecher

Norman Cousins stated, "During laughter, the human brain produces secretions which are morphine-like molecules, called endorphins and enkephalins." Research shows that a person's ability to tolerate pain is enhanced after exposure to humorous movies. Other studies have shown a decrease in the request for pain medications following comedy movies which the participants select. When people go to Dale Anderson, M.D. with various aches and pains, he frequently will write a laughter prescription, which says, "Stand in front of the mirror for fifteen seconds twice a day, and get into the most gut-wrenching, belly-shaking, gas-passing laughter that you can." He tells them to either "laugh 'til the cows come home or until they leak." The point is that the best laughter to trigger the pain relievers needs to be as hearty as possible.

The catecholamines released by the body during laughter stimulate the production of endorphins. While some feel that laughter works through diversion or distraction from the pain, others feel that the endorphins, which are similar in chemical structure to morphine, actually cause the same chemical reactions in the body as a pain antagonist like morphine. As a result of her research study, Ruth Davidhizer states that the betaendorphins which are secreted during laughter affect pain-receptor cells at the nerve endings and thereby reduce pain sensations. Perhaps the effects are actually a combination of chemicals and diversion.

Laughter can be a powerful tool to reduce pain. We must believe that it will work, then make it happen.

Ann Weeks, D.N.S., is a nurse family therapist and past-president of the Association for Applied and Therapeutic Humor. Both she and

Dr. Anderson have written about other ways to raise or lower endorphins. The level of these chemicals in the body can be raised through:

- Exercise
- Eating
- Pleasurable experiences through the senses of sight, touch, taste, sound, and smell
- Positive connections
- Recognition
- Positive attitudes
- Initial stages of acute pain or stress

In these initial stages, the body produces extra endorphins to deal with the pain or stress. If the pain or stress is not relieved, it becomes chronic, thereby depleting the supply of extra endorphins. The body's supply lessens during chronic pain or stress, as well as from poor posture, poor physical condition, and people or thoughts which produce a negative feeling.

## L  Lightens Stress

*With the fearful strain that is on me day and night,*
*if I did not laugh, I shall die.*

—Abraham Lincoln

Cortisol is a hormone associated with stress. Laughter decreases the amount of cortisol in the body. Laughter can also directly combat the muscle tension associated with stress. The catecholamines which are released during stress actually relax skeletal muscle tension, so the muscles cannot remain tight when laughing. People have often described getting weak from laughter. In one comic episode of Laurel and Hardy, two people were attempting to carry a mattress up some stairs. They kept laughing so hard and dropping the mattress that they were finally too weak to accomplish the task.

## I  Increases Brain-cell Function

*The body manifests what the mind harbors.*

—Jerry Augustine

Enjoying and laughing at humorous situations requires both sides of the brain. Using these cells in this way stimulates them and can improve their functioning. It is said that man can lose what he does not use. Many cells and areas of the brain have not been fully developed and have not achieved their full potential. By enjoying humor and laughing, these cells can be stimulated for more productivity. Sven Svebak reports greater co-ordination between the right and left hemispheres following a laughter experience, producing a more holistic consciousness.

## T  Tickles The Funny Bone

*One of the best things people can have up their sleeves is a funny bone.*

—Richard L. Weaver II

Patch Adams, M.D., founder of the Gesundheit Institute, states that humor and fun are equal partners with love as key ingredients for a healthy life. Humor and fun will be present in one's life when something tickles the funny bone. What makes us laugh is unique to each person. The mirthful spirit which tickles the funny bone has the power of increasing one's pep and vitality.

## Y   Yields Healthful Rewards

*Happy people generally don't get sick.*
—Bernie Siegel, M.D.

Laughing to the point of tears yields healthful rewards. The tears are cleansing and release some accumulated toxins, steroids, and hormones which are associated with times of stress. Other healthful rewards are part of the first six letters of the acronym, V-I-T-A-L-I-T-Y.

A mirthful spirit and laughing, which are the emotional and physical responses to humor, spark and energize our vitality. As we've learned from our own experiences and from research participants: "Laughter makes me feel good and keeps me going.... Laughter is a necessity for relaxing and easing tension."

*Vitality! That's the pursuit of life, isn't it?*
—Katherine Hepburn

# 4

## Laughing For Sociability

*A smile is the light in your face to let people know you are at home.*

—Allen Klein

Humor, laughter, and a mirthful spirit provide many psychological and sociological benefits. It can add sparkle to an individual. This, in turn, radiates to others and helps build bridges to create meaningful relationships with other people. Thus, social bridging or sociability, along with vitality, are the foremost benefits of laughter according to our research participants. We illustrate the benefits of laughter for sociability with the acronym S-O-C-I-A-L-I-Z-I-N-G.

**S** *Sets the stage*

**O** *Offsets life's upsets*

**C** *Creates contagious mirth*

**I** *Inspires self-esteem; Instills confidence*

**A** *Adds sparkle*

**L** *Lubricates and balances life*

**I** *Ignites cohesiveness*

**Z** *Zings zest into conversations*

**I** *Increases curiosity and flexibility*

**N** *Nourishes hope; Neutralizes negativity*

**G** *Garnishes life; Gives meaning to life*

## S   Sets The Stage

*A smile is the shortest distance between two people.*

—Victor Borge

Having a mirthful spirit and using laughter set the stage for sociability.

The atmosphere is relaxed. Mark Twain once said, "The human race has only one really effective weapon, and that's laughter. The moment it arises, all our harnesses yield, all our irritations and resentments slip away, and a sunny spirit takes their place." Smiling and laughter have been called the universal language, because the intent is understood in any language.

Humor and laughter are useful in establishing rapport, breaking the ice, encouraging trust, and reducing fear. Davidhizer showed that jokes at the start of a meeting can reduce tension and boost morale. Mirth and laughter set the stage for positive interactions.

## O   Offsets Life's Upsets

*Trouble knocked on the door, but hearing laughter, hurried away.*

—Benjamin Franklin

A mirthful spirit and laughter help to keep things in perspective. It enables one to step aside from the upsets to see something positive during an otherwise miserable time. It is said that there is always both negative and positive in every situation. Both are needed for survival on earth. If one totally blocks the experiences of grieving or feeling pain, it may have the effect of also blocking the ability to really feel good about something. Grief and pain are normal occurrences in life, and should not be avoided; they need to be accomplished. However, one can choose whether to focus on the negative or the positive. Focusing on the negative soon makes one feel that way. It makes one feel down and unhappy. Focusing on the positive makes one feel better and enhances the mirthful spirit within.

Herth states that laughter increases the ability to cope with unbearable situations. Maria Nemeth found a positive relationship between the use of appropriate humor and the reduction of anxiety. George Vaillant noted that humor is one of four mature coping mechanisms available to a person for successfully dealing with difficult situations. The other three factors are sublimation, altruism, and suppression. As so aptly stated previously by a research participant, laughter is a way to dump our emotional garbage and live across it.

## C  Creates Contagious Mirth

*Smiling is infectious, I catch it like the flu. I share that smile as I pass it on to you.*

—Adapted by Edna Thayer

Mirth is contagious. People who see someone smile often feel like smiling in return. It can have a rolling snowball effect and gather momentum as it is passed from one to another. Humor builds relationships and decreases the distance between people. Many writers describe laughter as an infectious social experience which tends to foster mirthfulness.

## I  Inspires Self-esteem; Instills Confidence

*Laughing deeply is living deeply.*

—Milan Kundera

Provine says that laughter is psychologically linked with self-esteem. Several of our research participants used laughter to enhance their own self-esteem. Some describe laughter as a defense mechanism in response to a teasing situation, which in turn helps to diminish the amount of teasing.

One example of the relationship between humor and self-esteem happened in 1957. David was embarking on a blind date with Edna, who had just ended a relationship because she believed her friend was too self-conscious about his balding and receding hairline. His apparent loss of self-esteem had negatively colored the interactions between them. Imagine Edna's surprise when David appeared, also with a receding hairline and starting to turn bald. All doubts were washed away when David firmly shook Edna's hand and said, "My name is Thayer; it rhymes with hair which I don't have much of," as he pointed to his hair. David has a marvelous sense of humor, and he was able to joke about something over which no one has control and turn it into a positive emotion. Any correlation between the female in this story and one of the authors of this book is purely intentional. This couple celebrated 48 years of marriage in 2006. Self-esteem and confidence fostered by a sense of humor contribute to lasting relationships.

## A   Adds Sparkle

*It's better to laugh than to explode.*

—Research Participant

Humor brings the sparkle to life as it diverts stressful feelings of frustration, anxiety, anger, hostility, and fear. Laughter temporarily diverts underlying negative feelings to return the sparkle. Laughter and negative emotions are not compatible. The laughter acts as a pressure valve to release the feelings; it is not a "cure-all." Someone said it is like changing a baby. It makes things better for awhile, but until the underlying problem is resolved, the problem will come back.

## L   Lubricates And Balances Life

*Happiness is a way of travel; not a destination.*

—Roy Goodman

Henry Ward Beecher said that going through life without laughter is like riding through life without springs and lubricant in one's car. One is jolted by every pebble in the road. Humor is a "social lubricant" that eases tension and shyness. A mirthful spirit can provide that lubricant, which makes the journey through life a much smoother ride.

Humor serves a vital purpose of providing balance, equilibrium, perspective, and survival. The research participants declare that laughter and humor decrease their loneliness and anxiety and increase their feelings of well-being.

## I   Ignites Cohesiveness

*A joy that is shared is a joy made double.*

—English Proverb

Research participants describe laughter as "relationship building." Feeling a bond with other people can be helpful both personally and professionally.

Several studies show that social isolation is related to mental illness, physical illness, loneliness, and decreased independence. Most people would agree that a balance between time alone and time with other people is ideal. Laughter and humor initiate togetherness, warmth, and friendliness. The contagious social experience of laughter tends to show acceptance and create a common bond. A sense of belonging and cohesiveness is often an outcome of sharing laughter.

## Z Zings Zest Into Conversations

*I like the laughter that opens the lips and the heart.*
—Victor Hugo

Laughter brings forth the liveliness and spirit in a conversation. It zings zest into a social interaction.

## I Increases Curiosity And Flexibility

*Be flexible and you won't get bent out of shape.*
—Les Helms

Humor puts people at ease and promotes the expression and exchange of ideas. Having the right perspective can facilitate problem-solving, both among individuals and within a group.

Learning is enhanced when the body's natural chemicals of epinephrine, catecholamine, and dopamine are released through laughter. The result is increased alertness, increased short-term memory, and increased creativity.

## N Nourishes Hope; Neutralizes Negativity

*The pessimist sees the difficulty in every opportunity. The optimist sees the opportunities in every difficulty.*
—Lip Jacks

To nourish is to maintain or foster something. A mirthful spirit nourishes hope. Kaye Herth, Ph.D., describes hope as one of five beneficial functions of humor. The other four are connectedness, relaxation, perspective, and joy. Hope enables people to face realities of everyday existence. Provine states that humor is positively linked with optimism and negatively related to negative affect.

Besides the use of Vitamin C and laughter, Norman Cousins credited a positive attitude and hope with his recovery. In his book, *The Biology of Hope*, he shared an interesting story about hope with the comparison of the practice of two oncologists. One called his protocol for treating cancer EPOH, which refers to the first letters of the drugs which he used: Etoposide, Platinol, Oncovin, and Hydroxyurea. His patients had a 22 percent favorable response rate. The other doctor used the same drugs, but reversed the order of listing the drugs and referred to them by the letters HOPE. The favorable response rate increased to 74 percent for the patients whose doctor used the term HOPE with his prescribed protocol of drugs.

The emerging field of psychoneuroimmunology supports the view that different components of the immune system are suppressed by anxiety, depression, negative moods, helplessness, hopelessness, pessimism, and loneliness. Positive moods and mental states can strengthen the immune system. Humor leading to a mirthful spirit and laughter can help maintain a positive mood on a day-to-day basis and nourish hope while it activates the immune system to improve the body's own ability to fight disease. By using the apothecary in the brain, one promotes the healing powers of the body.

When negativity is neutralized, the result is a more positive attitude. Several participants in our research study agreed that for them, a positive attitude was the most important ingredient in wellness.

## G   Garnishes Life; Gives Meaning To Life

*If each one lit one candle in their corner of the world,*
*what a bright world this would be.*

—Rev. Martin Luther King, Jr.

Just as garnish makes food more appetizing and appealing, a mirthful spirit garnishes or decorates life to make it more palatable and interesting. It gives extra meaning to one's daily existence. It makes life joyous and fun, melting away dullness and boredom. The ability to find enjoyment in the daily activities of life is enhanced with a mirthful spirit. A mirthful spirit and positive laughter form socializing connections among people. Laugh for sociability.

*He deserves paradise who makes his companions laugh.*

—Muhammad in *The Koran*

# Poetic Musing:
## From Mirth To Laughter To Wellness

I started today with a feeling of mirth.
It led to laughter and all that it's worth.
Why do mirth and laughter make me feel so great?
There are so many reasons to relate.

Laughing increases my physical vitality.
It makes me feel more alert and fosters creativity.
Jogging my diaphragm increases circulation,
While also increasing my oxygenation.

So I breathe in more air and my blood really moves,
Muscles relax and digestion improves.
During bouts of laughter, pain is decreased
Due either to diversion or the endorphins released.

Maintaining a mirthful perspective
Gives rise to being humor-selective.
Laughter is contagious
And may lead to being silly or outrageous.

Laughter enhances interactions leading to sociability.
It increases curiosity and flexibility.
Bonding, confidence, and self-esteem will increase
Due to the contagious nature of laughter's release.

Giving life to mirth nourishes hope,
Then I will have future ways to cope.
I know smiling is part of mirthfulness;
All of which leads me to enriched wellness.

# PART II

## Nurturing a Mirthful Spirit

## 5
*Cultivating a Mirthful Spirit for Yourself*

## 6
*Finding Mirth During Distress*

## 7
*Preventing Negative Teasing*

## 8
*Growing and Aging Mirthfully*

# 5

## Cultivating A Mirthful Spirit For Yourself

*The U. S. Constitution does not guarantee happiness, only the pursuit of it. You have to catch up with it yourself.*

—Benjamin Franklin

Mirth is a joyous feeling. Note that we use the words *mirth* and *joy* interchangeably. Why is it that two people can be in the same surroundings, and one may experience joy while the other may not feel mirthful? Our research participants told us the answer. The key is one's receptivity to the joyful moment. The particular ideas or events which trigger joy in a person are so variable and individual that it is impossible to prescribe one formula for happiness to serve everyone. The people in our study describe various ways of finding mirth and joy, as summarized by Edna Thayer in the following poem:

Some enjoy chattering with friends; others prefer solitude alone.
Some enjoy seeing places afar; others prefer the sanctity of home.

Some bring joy when they come to visit; others bring joy when they leave.
Some enjoy giving to others they know; many are joyous when they receive.

Some enjoy performing in a play; others enjoy watching the play or movie.
Some listen to classical or "golden oldies;" others think jazz or punk rock is groovy.

Some enjoy families and children and antics of pets.
Others think relaxing in a hammock is as good as it gets.

Some find merriment in their own embarrassing moments or incongruities in life.
Others prefer recalling times of happiness when not under strife.

Even though there is not just one prescription for sources of humor for all, there are some general guidelines for action which can be helpful. These are summarized in the acronym R-E-C-E-P-T-I-V-I-T-Y.

**R** *Recognize that laughter is beneficial*

**E** *Enjoy life's situations*

**C** *Capture the mirth of funny events and everyday happenings*

**E** *Exaggerate for fun*

**P** *Practice being mirthful*

**T** *Take time to laugh each day*

**I** *Interpret things literally*

**V** *View life optimistically*

**I** *Intentionally seek opportunities to laugh*

**T** *Turn negative situations into positive ones*

**Y** *Yield to the playful child within oneself*

## R  Recognize That Laughter Is Beneficial

*Happiness is the meaning and purpose of life.*

—Aristotle

Having trouble being mirthful? Having trouble letting out a giggle or belly laugh? Not seeing enough humor in life? We'll help with that. In the meantime, try just laughing for a few moments because laughing is healthy and good for you. Laughing is good exercise. You start the day by washing, brushing your teeth, taking your vitamins, and eating breakfast. Now laugh a bit. Here's our point again: Laughing contributes to wellness.

## E  Enjoy Life's Situations

*Some pursue happiness, others create it.*

—Anonymous

Try to find humor in life, in your everyday experiences. We have little control over much of what happens, so why gripe or grimace. We might as well laugh. Consider aging. What can you do? Find some humor. Accepting these situations with a mirthful spirit can provide a more joyful outlook to life. Two examples of seeing mirth in aging are:

> *A woman's husband was becoming very hard of hearing.*
> *One day they were driving to a nearby town, when she said,*
> *"Look, honey, there's a deer in the ditch."*
> *Her husband responded, "Mine do, too."*
> *Bewildered, she queried, "What did you think I said?"*
> *His response was, "Didn't you say your ears itch?"*

> *A gentleman who is becoming quite bald tells everyone*
> *that he has found the perfect cure for baldness. It is called*
> *Preparation H. No, it does not grow any more hair, it just*
> *shrinks the scalp to fit the hair that you have left.*

## C  Capture Mirth Of Funny Events

*Life is 10 percent what you make it,*
*and 90 percent how you take it.*

—Irving Berlin

Funny events happen often. Turn on your radar. Adjust your antennae. Look through new lenses. Be receptive to humor in everyday events. Examples follow relating to children, daily communications, and people's names.

The innocence of children often provides a wonderful source of mirth. Three examples are:

*A co-worker is starting to develop some wrinkles. Her grandchild looked at her one day and asked if God had made her skin too large for her body.*

*Or as put by Mary's four-year-old niece, "Grandpa, your skin doesn't fit you so good anymore."*

*Edna's three-year-old granddaughter, Allison, was at her house to try on a new Easter dress. Edna asked Allison if she needed help changing clothes. She replied that she didn't need any help, she gets dressed all by herself now. By this time, she was stripped to her underpants and Edna noticed that she was wearing two pair. Edna asked why she wore two underpants. She replied, "Mommy told me to put on a clean pair each day. The one underneath is from yesterday, and the top one is from today."*

Daily communication can often have enjoyable double meanings. Can you imagine two nearby towns, one named Fertile and the other Climax? Can you imagine laughing at a newspaper headline reporting a terrible accident:

*Fertile Woman Killed in Climax.*

People's names can also provide a source of merriment. I laughed heartily at a recent convention. Helen Hunt was working at the "Lost and Found" table. At the start of one session, an announcement was made:

Anyone who has lost a pearl earring can go to Helen Hunt for it.

## E   Exaggerate For Fun

Make light of situations by exaggerating.

*When waiting at a stop sign for a particularly long line of traffic, the driver of the car said, "I didn't know they had a parade today."*

*When quizzed about exercising, an obese lady answered, "I quit jogging because it was bad for my health. My thighs rubbed together so hard that my underwear caught fire."*

*I waited so long in line to renew my driver's license that
I needed to shave again before they snapped my picture.*

## P    Practice Being Mirthful

*Laugh and the world laughs with you;
frown and you frown alone.*

—Robert Brody

Children laugh more, smile more, and play more than adults. Perhaps adults are out of practice. Joel Goodman has made it his life's work to promote humor through his Humor Project, Inc. He recommends that people rediscover the "elf" in yourself. He encourages people to use the five Ps: practice, practice, practice, practice, practice. Practice until humor becomes a habit, a natural part of the elf in yourself.

## T    Take Time To Laugh Every Day

*The most wasted day of all is that on which
we have not laughed.*

—Sebastian Chamfort

If you have not laughed during the day, then purposefully seek something funny to end the day. It could be a television program, a book, a video, funny friends or neighbors, or just purposefully reflecting on a fun time.

## I    Interpret Things Literally

Many words have more than one meaning. Taking the English language literally is a source of fun. Examples are:

*The gowns worn by patients in the hospital intensive
care units are often quite skimpy. That is why it is called,
"ICU."*

*Think about the hospital delivery room door that says,*
*"Push," or the urology nurse who answers the phone, "Can*
*you hold?"*

## V   View Life Optimistically

*Nothing is good or bad, but thinking makes it so.*

—Shakespeare

There is happy and sad, good and bad, positive and negative in every situation. One can often determine one's level of mirthfulness by determining one's focus. Buddha said, "Your life is what your thoughts make it." Highlighting the joys in one's life and looking at life optimistically make for a more mirthful spirit.

## I   Intentionally Seek Opportunities To Laugh

*Misery comes free.*
*Joy, fun, and laughter take planning.*

—C. W. Metcalf

*Life itself cannot give you joy*
*unless you really will it.*
*Life just gives you time and space.*
*It's up to you to fill it.*

—Chinese Proverb

Blessed are those who can find joy and happiness in daily life events. And blessed is a mirthful spirit, for it is contagious and can spread from one joyful person to another.

The Red Hat Society is a sparkling example of the power of purposefully seeking fun. When one of her friends turned 50, Sue Ellen Cooper decided to give her a whimsical gift. She framed a copy of the poem, "When I Grow Old, I Shall Wear Purple," and bought a red hat as a decorating idea to place on the wall next to the framed picture. It was such a hit with her group of friends that she continued to give this gift as others turned 50. Soon, there was a group of women who owned red hats, and they decided to buy purple outfits to wear with the hats and go out for tea. Thus began the Red Hat Society. It was so delightful that it spread like wildfire across the entire United States and into other countries. Five years later, in 2005, there were over 65,000 chapters. Fun is the glue that bonds these women. Having fun is a noble purpose for any group.

## T   Turn Negative Situations Into Positive

*Laughter is the best balance wheel in life.*
*It reminds us that there is a lot of joy in the world, not just a dark side.*

—Research Participant

The letter "V" of the acronym R-E-C-E-P-T-I-V-I-T-Y talks about viewing life positively. This letter "T" goes one step further to encourage people to turn negative situations into positive ones. It takes rain to make a rainbow. Find the bright side, the silver lining, and the golden glow of humor. No one ever injured his eyesight by looking at the bright side of things.

> *Years ago, Edna's grandparents, a farm couple from Minnesota, were entertaining relatives from Illinois. The evening was spent playing cards and having a good time. When the farmer awoke early in the morning to milk his cows, he found that the relatives had played a practical joke on him by tying his milk stool to the highest pinnacle of the barn. He told his wife that he did not know what to do because he could not milk*

*his cows without the stool, and he did not think he was agile
enough to retrieve the stool himself. The wife suggested that
he go back to bed and she would take care of it. She awak-
ened the relatives and said that her husband was sick in bed
and could they possibly milk the cows for him that morning.
They obliged her, got dressed, retrieved the milking stool, and
milked the cows. When they returned to the house, the farmer
was seated at the kitchen table eating breakfast while having
the last laugh.*

*A woman lost her credit cards but the husband was reluctant
to report it because the thief was charging less on the cards
than his wife did.*

## Y   Yield To The Playful Child Within

*Play is the work of children.*

—Rena Wilson

Be playful. Be childlike. Regain the playfulness of youth. Playfulness needs
to continue forever. As adults regain the playfulness of their youth, the mirthful spirit within will emerge. One does not need to be continuously laughing
to enjoy healthful benefits. Just having a mirthful spirit is beneficial.

Okay, now you are more receptive to humor, laughter, joy, and mirth.
If you do not create the humor itself, where does it come from? Benjamin
Franklin stated that "Happiness consists more in small pleasures that occur
every day than in great pieces of good fortune that happen but seldom."
What are the small pleasures and happenings occurring in your life? The
best sources are those that occur naturally, being receptive to finding joy
and mirth in the life around us. Sometimes it may be advantageous to
provide a booster shot to one's mirthful spirit by seeking opportunities to
have fun and laugh. Whether occurring naturally or purposefully, these
stimuli are "happenings." The acronym H-A-P-P-E-N-I-N-G-S may help
you notice, be more receptive, and become mirthful.

**H** *Happy occasions, celebrations*

**A** *Animals, birds, pets*

**P** *Printed material*

**P** *Performances*

**E** *Electronic media*

**N** *Neighbors, family, friends*

**I** *Incongruity*

**N** *Nostalgia, reminiscing*

**G** *Grandchildren and other children*

**S** *Self*

## H  Happy Occasions, Celebrations

*Shared laughter is love made audible.*

—Izzy Gesell

Happy occasions and celebrations spark mirth, joy, and fun. Celebrations by definition are festive, joyous, and uplifting. Celebrate birthdays, weddings, anniversaries, and special holidays. Recognize life's achievements like graduations, promotions, and retirements. Celebrate with neighbors, friends, relatives, and family. Create traditions for celebrating holidays, create happy times at parades or athletic events.

## A  Animals, Birds, Pets

*Animals are such agreeable friends –*
*They ask no questions, they pass no criticism.*

—George Eliot

The antics of animals, birds, and pets of all kinds can bring endless joy to observers. Whether you love animals or not, there is a simple warm joy in watching squirrels scamper up and down trees, dogs fetch, cats pounce, and the like. We need only be observant.

## P   Printed Material

*Every man who knows how to read has it*
*in his power to magnify and to multiply the ways in*
*which he exists, and to make his life significant,*
*full, and interesting.*

—Aldous Huxley

While mainstream media appears to be strongly tilted toward the negative and sensational, *Happy News* is an example of a positive approach to news. It is the brainchild of Byron Reese, chief executive of Austin, Texas-based PageWise Inc., which publishes several how-to and advice web sites. Reese launched *Happy News* in July, 2005, to balance the onslaught of stories about war, crime, and natural disasters found in mainstream media. Examples of headlines from *Happy News* include: "Emily, the stowaway cat, is coming home," an item about a Wisconsin tabby who got stuck in a cargo container and wound up in France, and "Washington Grape Growers Reap Record Harvest." Coverage of the war in Iraq might be limited to ways in which the Marines celebrated Thanksgiving and volunteers sending teddy bears to Iraqi children. *Happy News* and other sources of mirthful printed materials are found in the "Resources" section of the Appendices. You do not need *Happy News*, however, to find happiness in reading. A good book or diverting magazine can also do the trick.

## P   Performances

*The cinema has no boundary; it is a ribbon of dreams.*

—Orson Wells

Performances include sporting events, movies, plays, concerts, and videos. You can watch or participate. Since there are many choices, choose wisely. For example, if you seek mirth and joy, then perhaps you want to avoid horror movies.

## E   Electronic Media

*A young child was overheard saying the Lord's Prayer as: "And lead us not into temptation; but deliver us some e-mail."*

The influence of electronic media is everywhere. Electronic media includes television, movies, DVDs, videos, video games, computer programs, arcade games, music CDs or MP3s. A joke relating to the electronic age follows:

*An elderly gentleman was having coffee in a restaurant with some friends. He became bored with the discussion of such things as computers, cell phones, and other electronic equipment which he did not own, so he decided to take a break and go to the bathroom. Upon return, his friends at the table began to laugh, and he realized that he was bringing a trail of toilet paper with him. He lightened the situation by saying, "Oh, I must be receiving a fax."*

People we interviewed report that select programs on television bring joy. There was some concern that not all programs are funny or even fun to watch anymore. Again, choose carefully.

The use of the computer provides a whole new source of jokes. Some spend hours on the computer sharing jokes and stories with other friends. This is especially helpful for those who have limited mobility and limited access to other sources of joy.

## N   Neighbors, Family, Friends

*The supreme happiness of life is the conviction that we are loved.*

—Victor Hugo

To spend time with people who love us and care about us is one of life's supreme joys. Of course, not every person is a source of joy. Avoid those who dim your enthusiasm and darken your skies. Be intentional and selective when you choose your company. When it is not possible to choose the participants in a social group, choose your attitudes and reactions to the people who affect you negatively.

## I   Incongruity

*Try as hard as we may for perfection, the net result of our labors is an amazing variety of imperfections.*

—Samuel McChord Crothers

Incongruity refers to something that happens unexpectedly. It catches you off guard. Sometimes it is a source of embarrassment at the time. It can be as simple as tripping or as broad as arriving at a formal dinner party that you thought was a costume party. Looking for humor in an incongruous event can be a source of mirth if you are receptive. Laughter can also reduce the embarrassment of mistakes and awkward moments. Most comics thrive on finding humor in incongruous moments. Just thinking about Abbott and Costello, the Three Stooges, Laurel and Hardy, Lucille Ball, Bill Cosby, or Jerry Seinfeld may bring a smile to your face.

## N   Nostalgia, Reminiscing

*The test of enjoyment is the remembrance which it leaves behind.*

—Logan Pearsoll Smith

Reminiscing about nostalgic moments is a source of joy and mirth: your first bicycle, your first kiss, your first child, that job promotion, that funny moment, that surprise. Recall pleasant memories to enhance your mirthful spirit. Review your diary. Think about your mementos. Look at your photo albums. These will help you recall special moments. Ask your family and friends. At the next family anniversary or birthday celebration ask participants to share their favorite memory of the anniversary couple or birthday celebrant. Wedding and holiday gatherings provide a similar opportunity to share favorite remembrances from past celebrations and events. Or just relax, close your eyes, and think back to fun times.

## G  Grandchildren And Other Children

*If I had known how much fun grandchildren would be,*
*I would have had them first.*

—Mark Twain

Observing the antics of children can make you more joyful. If you do not have grandchildren or children to observe, then walk past a school yard or playground. Volunteer to work with children. For example, many schools have a program where older adults work with elementary children who are learning to read.

## S  Self

*Happy is the person who can laugh at himself.*
*He will never cease to be amused.*

—Habib Bourguiba

Laughing at yourself and with yourself is a great gift. You can grow from the experiences, too. Embarrassment is a terrific way to get a good laugh, relieve tension, and build good relationships. An example follows:

> *I (Edna) decided to visit a new Wal-Mart store that had opened in the area. When I arrived at the store, somehow I did not notice the large entrance. All I saw was the little half-door that was used to return carts to the building. Being a short person, I ducked and entered the store through this half door. Little did I realize that I had been observed by one of my co-workers. This incident was quickly shared back at my work setting, providing many chuckles as well as being used as an anecdote at my retirement party.*

Being able to laugh at yourself is a natural, spontaneous way of sharing with others and keeping things light and open. If you can laugh at yourself, then you are likely confident, positive, and mirthful.

So with R-E-C-E-P-T-I-V-I-T-Y to H-A-P-P-E-N-I-N-G-S in your life, let's think about intentionally incorporating humor and laughter into your personal and family life to facilitate a mirthful spirit. Being intentional includes:

- Asking yourself if you have laughed today.

- Smiling at people you meet, even if you do not know them.

- Smiling and laughing at every opportunity.

- Pausing to enjoy the smiles, funny expressions and happiness of children.

- Trying to make at least one other person smile each day.

- Making time on your schedule for mirth, just as you would make time to eat and brush your teeth.

- Laughing as hard as possible for 15 seconds, twice a day.

- Reading a favorite cartoon or joke each day.

- Making a "joy list" of things that bring you mirth and joy and then purposefully doing or enjoying something from the list each day.

- Making a "joy bag" of funny glasses, silly putty, bubbles, slinkies, happy toys, fun books, happy faces, or whatever else might foster a quick mirthful moment for yourself or others. Use the item alone or with family and friends when in need of a lift.

- Keeping a "fun file" of cartoons, drawings, sayings, clippings, photos, and such. Keep these at hand, in a notebook, or on a bulletin board or refrigerator to create a humor corner.

- Doing small favors for friends, neighbors, and family.

- Including humorous gifts for special occasions, such as a dozen Cheerios in a plastic bag labeled "dieter's donuts for the perpetual dieter," or an old pair of sun glasses with empty prescription bottles hot-glued to them and labeled "prescription sun glasses."

- Taking time each day, perhaps at an evening family meal, to have each person talk about what happened during that day to make him or her smile. It's good for digestion.

- Using and displaying around the house, fun objects, such as a hand mirror that laughs, a pepper shaker that says, "Ah-Choo," accompanied by a salt shaker that says, "Bless you," or cups or refrigerator magnets with whimsical sayings.

- Taking a "pleasure pause," a break in the day to lift your spirits with anything that brings you a little pleasure. Take a "mini vacation" through a quick daydream or enjoy a peaceful walk. The delight of such activity is captured in the following poem adapted by Edna Thayer from a "Garden Bench":

*I love to walk with grandpa; he takes short steps like mine;*
*He's never in a hurry; he seems to take his time.*
*We gather stones and pick up sticks, while he talks to me—*
*And listens to my every word with looks of joy and glee.*

*Your receptivity to humor is the single most important factor in promoting a mirthful spirit.* We think everyone needs a positive attitude to seek and find the joys of life. Remember, you do not have to look far. Occasions or opportunities for mirth and joy abound. Even so, you cannot go wrong by purposefully and intentionally seeking sources of joy.

*Then I commanded mirth because people have no better thing, under the sun than to eat, drink, and to be merry.*

—Ecclesiastes 8:15

# 6

## Finding Mirth During Distress

*Happiness and trouble stand at everyone's gate.*
*Yours is the choice which you will invite in.*

—Anonymous

Receptivity is the most important variable in determining one's response to humor. People vary in the types of jokes to which they respond mirthfully. People also vary in whether or not they will respond at all, depending upon other circumstances at the moment. When feeling distress, people do not feel like laughing. The acronym D-I-S-T-R-E-S-S illustrates some examples.

**D** *Detrimental humor*

**I** *Illness and injury*

**S** *Sorrow and loss*

**T** *Tragic world events*

**R** *Ridiculing, teasing, bullying*

**E** *Emotional struggles, depression*

**S** *Sad disappointments*

**S** *Serious times*

## D  Detrimental Humor

*Oh, a trouble's a ton, or a trouble's an ounce, or a trouble is what you make it, And it isn't the fact that you're hurt that counts, but only how you take it.*

—Edmund Vance Cooke

Humor is detrimental when it causes more harm than good, when it hurts instead of heals, when it makes people feel worse instead of better. Detrimental, negative humor comes at the expense of others. While not all people react the same way to inappropriate humor, and some can see the humor in the joke and not take offense, detrimental humor is risky to use in a group where one does not know each individual well. We identify eleven categories of inappropriate humor by using the acronym d-e-t-r-i-m-e-n-t-a-l. An example of a short joke is given for each category, attempting to select some which are mild enough not to be offensive. If this goal is not accomplished, please consider it as an example of the fine line between good humor and inappropriate humor.

**d**  *Derogatory political jokes*

**e**  *Ethnic, cultural jokes*

**t**  *Taunting, sarcasm, put-downs*

**r**  *Religious jokes*

**i**  *Inside jokes*

**m**  *Mortifying jokes*

**e**  *Estrogen/androgen jokes, otherwise known as sexist jokes*

**n**  *Negative jokes*

**t**  *Timing-inappropriate jokes*

**a**  *AT instead of WITH jokes*

**l**  *Lewd jokes*

Derogatory political jokes: Jokes about any political party or any branch of the government may be inappropriate because they might be offensive to someone else's convictions. These jokes are uncomplimentary and often are a form of laughing AT instead of WITH others. The word derogatory as used in this example is intended to be inclusive of all types of political jokes such as:

> *Some say that election year is that period of time when politicians get free speech confused with cheap talk.*

> *A skillful politician is one who can stand up and rock the boat and make you believe he is the only one who can save you from the storm.*

> *Beware of politicians who claim they'll build you a pie in the sky; they're only using your own dough.*

Ethnic and cultural jokes: Ethnic jokes probably exist for every nationality around. In Minnesota, perhaps the most common ethnic jokes are the Ole and Lena jokes about Norwegians. Other examples of cultural jokes are those that poke good-natured fun between residents of rival states. Examples of cultural jokes include:

> *People from Iowa say, "The best thing to come out of Minnesota to Iowa is Interstate Highway 35."*

> *Minnesota has four seasons: almost winter, winter, still winter, and road construction.*

> *Driving is better in Alaska in the winter because the pot holes are packed with snow.*

> *A man from Texas rode into town on Friday. Three days later he rode out of town on Friday. How can this be? His horse was named Friday.*

> *Two Eskimos became chilly in their kayak, so they lit a fire. The craft sank which proves: "You can't have your 'kayak' and 'heat' it, too."*

Taunting, sarcasm, put-downs: Some comedians, notably Don Rickles, have become famous for a particular style of humor composed mainly of sarcastic put-downs. Poking fun at another's age is included in this category. While it may be funny, there are those who find it offensive. It is even more offensive when the target of the joke takes the joke personally.

"Roasting" is a form of laughing AT and typically identifies faults and traits of a person which can be seen as a target for laughter. "Toasting" on the other hand may include humor, but it is done in a way that laughs WITH a person and builds rather than tears down the person's self-esteem. Two examples of put-downs taken from a typical roast are:

> *Our guest of honor is living proof that having a goal, a dream, and struggling hard to attain it, doesn't always work.*

> *He's afraid of his own shadow—and for good reason. It looks just like him.*

Religious jokes: Religious jokes are sometimes okay when told about one's own religion to another person of the same religion. It becomes offensive when one uses the joke as a put-down for a religion other than one's own, especially when told to a person of the other religion. Janet Letnes Martin and Suzann Johnson Nelson wrote a delightful book comparing Catholics and Lutherans entitled *They Glorified Mary and We Glorified Rice*. Two of the comparisons from the book are: "They chanted and we could read music," and "They had sextons and we had no sex at all." Other examples of religious jokes are:

> *It wasn't the apple in the tree that caused the problem in the Garden of Eden, it was the "pair" on the ground.*

> *A man was hired to paint a tall church. Just as he was completing the steeple, he began to run out of paint. Not wanting to climb all the way down, he decided to add a little thinner to the paint to make it stretch. Just then the thunder rolled and a loud voice from the sky boomed, "Repaint, repaint, and thin no more."*

Inside jokes: Inside jokes are those which are only understood by the participants of the situation or joke. This type of joke is fine if it is used when only those people who understand are present. The problem comes when an inside joke is used with others present. Those who do not understand are left out of the conversation and left out of the humor. It is almost impossible to give an example of an inside joke that would be understood by others. However, there is one example that can be explained. When Edna was a nurse executive, she was known for her unusually messy desk. At one banquet, she was presented with a plaque which read:

*Don't mess up the things on this desk. You'll only confuse me and screw up my whole world.*

Mortifying jokes: Mortification refers to a collection of humor that is derived from situations that bring shame, humiliation, chagrin, and embarrassment. Some people with a good sense of humor are able to turn embarrassing situations into a humorous anecdote. Others find no humor at all in this type of situation when it happens to them. A true example of a potentially mortifying situation is:

*When Edna was a college professor, she was walking across the campus from the parking lot to the classroom building when an extremely strong gust of wind came along and blew the wig right off her head. She wondered who was watching as she ran to retrieve the wig, while the wind kept blowing it further away.*

Estrogen/Androgen jokes, otherwise known as sexist jokes: Estrogen and androgen refer to the hormones which determine female or male characteristics. These terms in the acronym are used to describe sexist type jokes about females or males. Sometimes it may be acceptable for people to tell jokes about their own gender, but it is considered a put-down or even a form of harassment to tell the joke about people of the opposite gender. An example of a sexist joke is the one told by a female employee:

*Of course I don't work as hard as the men, I get it right the first time.*

Negative jokes: Negative type jokes are those which use a negative thought for the punch line. Examples are:

*The light at the end of the tunnel will be turned off until further notice.*

*If you're not the lead dog, the view never changes.*

Typically, this type of joke is not too offensive, except that for every negative thought one has it takes four positive thoughts to counteract the negative one and keep thinking positively. Robert H. Schuller, founder of the Crystal Cathedral in Garden Grove, California, offers four copyrighted examples for maintaining a positive attitude:

- *Turn your scars into stars.*

- *Tough times never last, but tough people do.*

- *Inch by inch, anything's a cinch.*

- *Every problem is an opportunity waiting to be discovered.*

Timing-inappropriate jokes: As the categories under the acronym D-I-S-T-R-E-S-S reveal, there are times when it may be inappropriate to use humor. Others may not be receptive to the mirthful attempt. However, even in times of distress, humor may be appropriate and welcomed by the individual if done with compassion and sincerity. Usually one needs to take the cue from the other person. For example, it would not be appropriate to start cracking jokes at the visitation for a deceased loved one. However, if the family recalls fun times and happy moments from the past, it is acceptable to laugh with them, and may even help them through their grieving process to replace the sadness of the moment with happier thoughts from the past.

AT instead of WITH jokes: It is never appropriate to laugh AT others. In fact, it is dangerous to laugh at others. If a person starts to laugh at whatever caused the situation, then it is appropriate to join in the laughter WITH that person. Sometimes in a close relationship a person may give permission to laugh AT certain characteristics, such as one's ethnic origin, while considering other topics off-limits. If there is a mutual understanding that certain topics are okay as a source of laughter, then it is okay to share jokes about these topics. Laughing at others is having fun at the expense of another person without their permission. It is a form of teasing and taunting.

Lewd jokes: Lewd humor is vulgar or sexually explicit. For some reason many comics today think lewd humor is a necessary ingredient for entertainment. However, there are many who do not appreciate such humor. It is much safer to find jokes which do not depend on lewd language to be funny. An example of a joke that could be considered sexually explicit is:

> *After 47 years of marriage, my husband and I finally achieved sexual compatibility last Friday night. — We both had a headache.*

Detrimental, teasing jokes and sarcasm may sometimes be used between two people who know each other well, have given permission for use of these types of jokes, and who both enjoy the same type of humor. It should never be used with a group where one does not know what type of humor is acceptable to the others and what might be taken as a put-down.

One study finds that humor is related to trust. The following table is supported by several humor experts such as Anderson, Goodman, and Hageseth and summarizes the differences between helpful or healing humor and harmful humor:

| Helpful or Healing Humor | Harmful Humor |
| --- | --- |
| Bonds people and avoids offense | Divides people |
| Laughs at self or WITH others | Laughs AT others |
| Decreases tension | Increases tension |
| Builds confidence | Destroys self-worth |
| Involves others in enjoyment | Excludes others (inside jokes) |
| Heals the spirit | Hurts the spirit |
| Expressed with empathy | Expressed with arrogance |
| Honors one's faith as the source of joy | Ridicules righteousness |

It may not be easy to attempt to interrupt the negative humor. There is no one best way to do this. However, here are some helpful suggestions from Christian Hageseth M.D. First, evaluate the situation, the people involved, and the nature of the interaction in order to decide the next step. After evaluating the situation, decide if one of the following is appropriate:

- *Move from awareness to action.*
  Rather than just noticing negative humor and being offended, or watching others being offended, consider an approach which may be helpful.

- *Offer a different perspective.*
  Use a quotation which the person may not have considered. For example: "The ax forgets; the tree remembers." Or "Blowing out my candle won't always make yours shine brighter."

- *Use an "I" message.*
  Such as "I really do not want to hear a sexist joke" or "I think people might find ethnic comments indefensible." It may be necessary to walk away. This deflates the person who may then lose interest in telling the story.

- *Use silence.*
  After hearing the joke or story, do not respond to it. Silence becomes golden. This is very effective and makes your point memorably.

- *Request an explanation.*
  Ask the joke-teller to explain the meaning of the negative humor. Whenever one has to explain a joke, it is disarming to the teller, the joke loses its funniness, and the incongruity is destroyed.

Detrimental humor greatly inhibits one's receptivity to humor, yet such humor is within one's power to control. Let's return to the acronym D-I-S-T-R-E-S-S, and continue with the letter 'I'.

# I   Illness And Injury

*One cannot get through life without pain.*
*What we can do is choose how to use the pain life*
*presents to us.*

—Bernie S. Siegel, M.D.

People we interviewed described times of illnesses or injuries to themselves or their family or friends as quite distressing. They became less receptive to humor and mirth and more vulnerable to anxiety and fear. The mind and body are using energy to cope with the situation. However, many of the interviewees mentioned that humor sometimes helps them cope with such anxiety and distress and can be beneficial when used with caring and empathy. They went on to say:

- *I have a friend who has lupus, cancer, and fibromyalgia. She's still able to laugh even with many problems; it's probably what keeps her going.*

- *Laughter helps in relaxation.*

- *Laughter helps take your mind off some horrible things.*

- *Laughter helps one step aside of oneself, at least momentarily, to think of happier things.*

- *Laughter helps one not be so conscious of the body's problems.*

Kaye Herth studied the receptivity to humor during stages of illness of people over age 65. She found that all were receptive during the chronic or convalescent times of an illness. Those between 65 and 80 were not as receptive when the illness was in the acute stage. Those who were over 80 were receptive even when acutely ill. They reported that during an acute illness they most needed a strong sense of humor. Other supportive comments from her study for the use of humor during illness or injury include:

- *Humor is a reprieve from difficulties.*

- *Humor makes me forget my worries.*

- *Humor makes me feel relaxed all over.*

- *Humor restores my fighting spirit.*

- *Humor helps me feel more alive.*

- *Humor helps give a new view during illness, to help transcend from hopeless to hopeful.*

Use humor during times of illness or injury with caring and empathy, and only when the recipient gives a cue that he or she is ready for humor. Allen Klein states that the hardest thing one can do is smile when one is ill, in pain, or depressed, but the no-cost remedy is a necessary first step to start on the road to recovery.

# S   Sorrow And Loss

*You cannot prevent the birds of sorrow from flying over your head, but you can prevent them from building nests in your hair.*

—Chinese Proverb

There are many kinds of loss in one's life which can bring sadness and distress. It may be the death of a family member or friend. It may be the loss or decrease of some function of the body, such as an inability to walk or speak after a stroke. It may be the loss of a job or financial security. It may be the loss of a home or other personal belongings. Any type of loss can lead to sadness or distress and diminish one's receptivity to mirth and humor. Yet receptivity to humor can be helpful during these times.

In the event of a death, for example, replacing the sadness of the moment with happier memories of previous times can help someone with grieving. Grieving is a natural process and a task which must be accomplished to move forward with life. It can be made easier with a sense of mirth, remembering the joyful times. It is not uncommon to see remembrances of fun times tucked inside a coffin. Examples have included pheasant feathers for the hunter, farewell letters from grandchildren, a bottle of Tabasco sauce for the man who used it to flavor everything, and a picture of a joyful time to remember. Many churches now have turned funeral services into "Celebrations of Life" instead of a service of mourning for the dead. There will still be many tears, but they will be intermingled with pleasant memories of the deceased person's life.

Participants in our study mentioned how a sense of humor can help them accept whatever happens to them along life's way. Humor, mirth, and laughter help create an attitude of acceptance.

# T  Tragic World Events

*We deem those happy who from the experience*
*of life have learned to bear its ills,*
*without being overcome by them.*

—Juvenal

War, floods, hurricanes, tornadoes, 9/11, terrorism, the explosion of a shuttle hurtling into space—many participants in the study mentioned such events as examples of times when they did not feel like being joyful. People have empathy with the distress of those around them and in the world, even if it does not directly affect them. Just thinking about the distress caused by these situations can inhibit one's ability to be open and receptive to a mirthful spirit.

## R Ridiculing, Teasing, Bullying

*Unhappy is the man whom man can make unhappy.*

—Ralph Waldo Emerson

Ridiculing, teasing, and bullying are easier to give than to take. Such humor can seriously damage the target's self-esteem. Such humor creates victims and perpetrators. We devote the next chapter specifically to this topic because we are profoundly disturbed by the increasing violence and frequency of school shootings and youth suicides in recent years. Not all school tragedies have been connected to taunting and bullying, but such behavior is a significant factor in many cases of school violence and suicide.

## E Emotional Struggles, Depression

*Peace begins with a smile.*

—Mother Teresa

Emotional struggles—fear, anxiety, anger, depression—also inhibit one's receptivity to mirth. Depressed and anxious people tend to consider humor an example of inconsiderate disregard for their feelings. They may interpret an attempt at humor as further confirmation of their inadequacies.

However, Davidhizer and Bowen report that the use of humor with depressed patients, when used with sensitivity and when done with a skilled therapist, was highly successful. The ability to laugh appropriately in situations is one measure of healing in a depressed person.

## S   Sad Disappointments

*When one door of happiness closes, another opens; but often we look so long at the closed door, that we do not see the one which has been opened for us.*

—Helen Keller

When life's disappointments are met with sadness it becomes a source of distress which dampens one's mirthful spirit and one's ability to see situations as funny. Not all disappointments are sad. Sometimes a disappointment in life is actually a motivation to try harder to succeed. The disappointment can promote growth instead of distress.

## S   Serious Times

*To be able to concentrate for a considerable time, is essential to difficult achievement.*

—Bertrand Russell

Serious times are situations when one is focused on a physical or mental task and prefers to use one's energies and concentrations on that task without the interruption of humor. Huntley notes that when concentration is focused on problem-solving, humor and laughter may actually increase tension. She refers to these serious times as "untimely occasions for laughter." Be careful.

Distress is a time of great pain, anxiety, sorrow, or trouble. However, even during distressing times, a positive attitude and mirthful spirit can help people accept their circumstances, cope, and adapt.

*Life is not always what one wants it to be, but to make the best of it as it is, is the only way to be happy.*

—Jennie Jerome Churchill

# 7

# Preventing Negative Teasing

*Teasing is like a knife. It can provide either benefits or injuries—depending upon whether it is grasped by the handle or the blade.*

—Edna Thayer

Teasing can be beneficial or harmful, depending on how it is perceived by the person being teased. Even when teasing does not escalate to tragedy, it can silently diminish the target's self-esteem. We include this chapter as a response to the increasing number of school shootings and suicides.

Several retired adults who participated in our research studies vividly recall hurtful experiences of teasing from their youth. Teasing for them caused powerlessness, fear, anger, and distrust. Some recalled hurtful teasing which continued into adult life.

Teasing may be a source of affectionate, good-humored fun. Teasing may also be mean-spirited taunting. The following poem by Thayer distinguishes playful teasing from provocative taunting:

Teasing is lighthearted, playful, and fun;
Taunting is hurtful and harmful to one.

Teasing is intended to get persons to laugh WITH each other;
Taunting is one-sided where laughing is AT another.

Teasing maintains dignity and a spirit of reciprocal mirth;
Taunting humiliates, is cruel, and demeans one's self-worth.

Teasing stops when one senses it is not perceived in a playful way;
Taunting, causing distress, continues, and increases from day to day.

Playful teasing contributes to a mirthful spirit. However, a fine line distinguishes between good teasing and harmful teasing. Further, the person doing the teasing is not always aware of how it is being received by others.

The person who is being teased may be smiling outwardly while actually crying on the inside. Sometimes, teasing may start out in a fun-loving spirit, but the teaser may acquire a sense of power if the target reacts negatively and if observers reinforce the teaser. Such teasing becomes taunting—that is, teasing with the goal to annoy, to worry by jokes and ridiculous requests, to make fun of, or to bully. Such taunting amounts to mocking, ridiculing, insulting, or jeering another person, often by focusing on personal characteristics of the target which seem different, uncommon, or are misunderstood. These traits include race, religion, gender, sexual orientation, physical disabilities, mental characteristics, or mannerisms. You have seen it often. You have heard it often. Perhaps you, like most people, have even thought or said some similar things about people being short, being tall, being fat, being skinny, being a brain, being a dummy, being a "retard," being a loser, or having pimples. Verbal taunting is often the first step to physical taunting and bullying.

When the taunting and bullying persist, a victim may feel helpless and hopeless. A child may feel that the only escape is through death, such as in a school shooting, suicide, or both. A school shooting is often aimed at one's taunting attackers or kids from the same clique or group as the taunters. The U. S. Secret Service and the U. S. Department of Education studied 37 school shootings occurring in America between 1974 and 2000. The study concludes that many of the persons committing the shootings felt bullied, persecuted, or injured by others. These shootings are rarely sudden, impulsive acts. Rather, the acts are planned with a few others often knowing about the plans. In many cases other students were involved in the planning or the violent acts. At least one or more responsible adults had identified each attacker as someone in distress. These findings, appearing in *Threat Assessments in Schools: A Guide to Managing Threatening Situations and to Creating Safe School Climates (2004),* were reported in the October 4, 2005, issue of the *Minneapolis Star and Tribune* newspaper.

Suicides are as tragic as shootings. Suicide may follow a school shooting or stand alone as an escape from one's torment. Neil Marr and Tim Field coined the term "bullycide" to refer to suicides arising from bullying. Their book, *Bullycide, Death at Playtime: An Exposée of Child Suicide Caused by Bullying*, states that in 1999 one out of every thirteen U. S. high school students reported they had made a suicide attempt in the previous twelve months. In the year 2000, two thousand students succeeded. It is not known how many of these were bullycides, but some did leave a very clear note describing the details of bullying which had become too painful to tolerate any longer.

Recent statistics obtained on the Internet from the National Center for Injury Prevention and Control, a division of the Centers for Disease Control and Prevention (CDC 2006), www.cdc.gov, tell an equally tragic story.

- In 2003, 5570 young people ages 10 to 24 were murdered, an average of 15 each day. Firearms were the cause of death in 82 percent of these cases.

- In 2003, suicide was the third leading cause of death among young people ages 15 to 24. Of this total, 86 percent were male and 14 percent were female. Firearms were used in 54 percent of the youth suicides.

- In 2004, more than 750,000 young people ages 10 to 24 were injured from violent acts.

- In 2004, Grunbaum's survey showed that among students nationwide, 33 percent reported being in a physical fight one or more times in the 12 months preceding the survey.

In a 2001 CDC report an estimated 30 percent of 12- to 15-year-olds were involved in bullying difficulties. Feelings of hopelessness, loss of social relationships, and feelings of isolation and lack of connection with other people are risk factors related to the youth suicides reported by the CDC which could be related to bullying. Be on the lookout for these factors in the teens you know. Share mirth and optimism with them.

Hildegard Peplau, Ed.D., a well-known nurse educator and theorist referred to as the "mother of psychiatric nursing," taught that all behavior is meaningful, purposeful, and can be understood. Many mental health professionals support the similar notion that one's behavior at any given time is the best that the person is capable of at that time. Does that mean that the shootings and suicides are the best that person can do at that time? Probably yes, meaning that shootings and suicides appear "reasonable choices" within the confines of their thinking amid the persistent pain, embarrassment, shame, and anger engulfing the person at that time.

Does that mean the cycle leading to terror and tragedy cannot be broken? No. People can alter their environment and change the stimuli influencing their behavior. Changing the stimuli is an ongoing life-building process, and it needs to include all persons in the environment–the attacker, the victim, and the observers. This same rationale forms the basis for some of the counseling, therapy, and interventions. Ways to change the environment are listed using the acronym C-H-A-N-G-E  S-T-I-M-U-L-I.

**C** *Create opportunities to do good*

**H** *Help children help themselves*

**A** *Apply zero-tolerance rules in a thoughtful manner*

**N** *Nurture empathy*

**G** *Give lots of hugs, smiles, and good humor*

**E** *Enhance self-esteem*

**S** *Support children in making choices*

**T** *Teach friendship skills*

**I** *Involve yourself in efforts to make a difference*

**M** *Monitor exposure to electronic media*

**U** *Unite others in the efforts*

**L** *Live in the way that you teach; be a role model*

**I** *Instill a mirthful spirit*

## C  Create Opportunities To Do Good

*Give to the World the best that you can, and the best will come back to you.*

—Madeline Bridges

Teach children how to show caring and concern for others. It may be helping an elderly neighbor or relative mow a lawn; it may be playing bingo with the elderly in a nursing home; it may be including a younger brother or sister in some games; it may be giving a hug to someone; or it may be tending a garden or caring for animals. There are countless ways to show respect, care, and concern for others. Children who are given the opportunity and encouraged to do positive things for others not only feel good inside, but also learn empathy for other people. They develop a conscience that wants to help instead of hurt others.

## H  Help Children Help Themselves

*God helps them that help themselves.*

—Benjamin Franklin

Children need to learn to help themselves. Help children develop these life-long skills by encouraging children to do things for themselves and request help when needed. Offering help when requested is different from doing things for a child. This will help give the child the ability to respond in a helpful way if confronted with teasing or bullying.

One way to teach children to help themselves has been developed by the Creative Learning Ideas for Mind and Body (CLIMB) Theater in Inver Grove Heights, Minnesota. The organization presents anti-bullying skits to school children in urban and rural communities. Different scenarios are presented and children are taught the detrimental impact of bullying and ways to respond. It is a proactive approach to helping children make good choices for themselves.

# A   Apply Zero-tolerance Rules In A Thoughtful Way

*What we prepare for is what we shall get.*

—William Graham Sumner

*We set up harsh and unkind rules against ourselves.*
*No man is born without faults, that man is best*
*who has the fewest.*

—Horace

All 50 states now require schools to have policies, procedures, and programs in place that provide a safe environment for children. One of the goals is to eliminate bullying. This is a great plan as long as the zero-tolerance rules are implemented in a thoughtful way. It really does not make sense to expel a ten-year-old student who voluntarily turned in a plastic knife which she found in her lunch bag because she inadvertently took her mother's lunch sack instead of her own. One can only wonder about the wisdom of expelling a young Cub Scout who wore the same pants to school that he had worn the previous night to a den meeting, yet had forgotten to remove the scout knife from the pocket. While it is true that zero-tolerance means just that, what does this really teach children about rules and justice in the world? Sometimes it appears that the way these rules are enforced is through use of power that is almost as detrimental as bullying.

Hazing is a form of taunting and bullying that needs to be included in the zero-tolerance policies. Our culture often regards hazing as a fun rite of passage into a group. Young people have the need to belong, but it does not have to come at the expense of detrimental hazing. One example is an eighth-grade student who was fearful of starting ninth grade in a new school. He heard that it was common practice for upperclassmen to put the head of a freshman student in a toilet bowl, and flush the bowl, while holding the head in the swirling water. Each year one reads about college students who die from activities associated with peer pressure during initiation. There are ways to provide impressive, meaningful initiations into groups which can provide pleasant lasting memories. Applying zero-tolerance rules includes zero-tolerance for hazing.

We also believe that society must show zero-tolerance for ways in which contempt is shown for others. Barbara Colorosa, in her book *The Bully, The Bullied, and The Bystander,* states that bullying is not about conflict and anger. Rather she believes that physical and verbal bullying is the result of contempt. Programs need to show ways to promote respect and understanding for each other's differences, whether related to differences in race, religion, gender, sexual orientation, ethnic origin, physical attributes, or mental abilities. Since the bully may not understand or tolerate these differences, he or she may feel that the other person is inferior or unworthy of respect. Sometimes the bully actually portrays an air of superiority to cover up for feelings of inadequacy.

Educators need to develop programs that foster understanding, care, and respect instead of contempt. Some schools are including this type of program in their curricula. Three examples come from Minnesota. The first is Harriet Bishop Elementary School in Rochester, Minnesota, which has a program emphasizing "Life Skills to Live By." A different life skill is highlighted for each month of the school year. The nine selected for the 2005-2006 school year were: respect, responsibility, cooperation, self discipline, compassion, honesty, perseverance, acceptance, and generosity. A second example is Oak Ridge Elementary School in Sartell, Minnesota. This school has selected six traits or pillars to emphasize throughout the school year. The six are caring, citizenship, trustworthiness, respect, responsibility, and fairness. Both Dianne Dodge, principal of Harriet Bishop, and Randy Husmann, principal of Oak Ridge, report that teachers identified the life skills and character traits to be emphasized. The teachers at Harriet Bishop started with a list of 53 before it was narrowed down to the nine selected. One concrete way to measure success of the programs is the number of discipline referrals. Both principals reported in 2005 that there were fewer discipline referrals since launching their programs.

A third example is provided by the Greater Mankato Diversity Council (GMDC). According to founding Executive Director Marsha Danielson, GMDC is working diligently with everyone in public, private, and charter schools to focus on prejudice of all types among youth. By 2010 children in Mankato-area classrooms from kindergarten through senior year will have received an annual program on prejudice-reduction. Some of the facilitators of the program have experienced the effects of prejudice from people because of their differences—a young girl who was bullied daily for the way she dressed, a person confined to a wheelchair, and one who immigrated from another country. The young girl being bullied believes the persons doing the bullying have their own life issues, which may be low self-confidence and needs for attention. The program in Mankato evolved from a program used in Rochester, Minnesota, and is described in the website, www.mankatodiversity.com

Parents can play an important role by reinforcing these life skills outside of school. One example happened when a second-grade student came home all excited because he found three dollars in the school hallway. After much careful discussion between the mother and son, the son decided that this money could be someone's lunch money and that the best approach would be to bring the money to the school office in case someone would come to claim the lost money. After two weeks no one claimed the money, so the boy who turned it in was allowed to keep it. He made three dollars while learning a valuable lesson. The next day he found a penny in the mall parking lot and asked his mother where they could turn it in. The life lessons continued.

Dorothy Law Nolte, Ph.D., best summarized the value of teaching life skills at school and at home through her poem *Children Learn What They Live*. The author approved a shortened version, which is reprinted below with permission, excerpted from the 1998 book of the same title by Dorothy Law Nolte and Rachel Harris.

*If children live with criticism, they learn to condemn.*

*If children live with hostility, they learn to fight.*

*If children live with ridicule, they learn to feel shy.*

*If children live with shame, they learn to feel guilty.*

*If children live with encouragement, they learn confidence.*

*If children live with tolerance, they learn patience.*

*If children live with praise, they learn appreciation.*

*If children live with acceptance, they learn to love.*

*If children live with approval, they learn to like themselves.*

*If children live with honesty, they learn truthfulness.*

*If children live with security, they learn to have faith in themselves and in those about them.*

*If children live with friendliness, they learn the world is a nice place in which to live.*

We also believe: If children live with positive humor and laughter, they learn to be mirthful. Sharing and working together can foster positive change for everyone.

## N  Nurture Empathy

*Do unto others as you would have them do unto you.*

—The Golden Rule

Empathy is the ability to identify with another person, to enter and understand that person's feelings, emotions, and situation. Empathy helps children become sensitive to differences in others. Empathy helps children become caring, sensitive, and compassionate to other people's hurts and needs. Empathy helps a child develop a conscience that will not permit taunting and will not tolerate the taunting of others.

Adults can enhance and develop a child's sense of empathy. There are many opportunities along life's way to discuss how one feels following certain actions, as well as to discuss how one's actions might make another person feel. Discussion can then lead to how a child would wish to feel and what actions might bring about that response. The next step is to support and encourage the child to act in a way that would foster positive feelings and emotions.

## G  Give Lots Of Hugs, Smiles, And Good Humor

*To make the world a friendly place, one must show it a friendly face.*

—James Whitcomb Riley

Children learn that hugs, smiles, humor, and laughter are critical to feeling positive about themselves and to bonding with others. Children learn by observing these interactions between their parents and between other members of the family. Virginia Satir stated that people need four hugs a day to survive and twelve hugs a day to grow. When children witness the enjoyment of life and share laughter WITH others, they are more likely to want to foster this relationship with their peers, rather than laughing AT them.

Unfortunately, using hugs as a display of affection can have many meanings. Not all touch is good touch, and children need to be taught the difference between good or acceptable touch and bad or unacceptable touch. Some hugs are intrusive, and others may be an invitation to sexual relations, whether by mutual consent or by force. In many instances it has become inappropriate for non-family members to touch children. Even with this directive, elementary teachers can often give a hug by standing side by side with the student, instead of face to face. A more creative way to give a hug is through a large teddy-bear type puppet, in which both hands are inserted and the hug comes from the bear instead of the person. Good types of touch and hugs can be an indication that someone is being noticed, recognized, or liked. Such hugs can also express tenderness or offer comfort.

## E   Enhance Self-esteem

*It's difficult for people to keep a chip on their shoulder when they are allowed to take a bow.*

—Dian Ritter

*That kind of life is most happy which affords us the most opportunities of gaining our own esteem.*

—Samuel Johnson

*There is overwhelming evidence that the higher the level of self-esteem, the more likely one will treat others with respect, kindness, and generosity.*
*People who do not experience self-love have little or no capacity to love others.*

—Nathaniel Branden

Self-esteem is respect for oneself and thinking well of oneself. Self-esteem is fostered through positive reinforcement for successes and turning disappointments into challenges to succeed. Children who are loved unconditionally learn to like themselves. Deflating self-esteem is easy. Enhancing it takes focused concentration until it becomes a habit to talk with children in a way that shows respect and gratitude. For example, it is important to show appreciation and remember to thank children when they are helpful and tell them how helpful they were. Those with a strong sense of self-esteem tend to be competent in making positive choices when faced with bullying and other adversities.

## S   Support Children In Making Choices

*The strongest principle of growth lies in human choices.*
—George Eliot

*We choose our joys and sorrows long before we experience them.*
—Kahlil Gibran

Children who are given the opportunity to make choices learn to think for themselves and solve problems. Parents need to purposefully provide opportunities for their children to make choices early in life. One working mother needed to leave for work before her kindergarten child was awake to dress for school. The father had the responsibility of getting the child ready for school. In an effort to make this time run smoother in the morning, the mother set out seven sets of clothing on top of the dresser, from which the child could choose what to wear on any given day. This gave the mother peace of mind, knowing that the outfits would be coordinated and not clash. It also allowed for the child to develop some independence and make choices. Feeling successes in making these minor types of choices help children gain confidence when faced with making more major choices later in life. We agree with Colorosa that making little choices early in life may help provide the groundwork for a student to effectively deal with bullying.

## T  Teach Friendship Skills

*The only way to have a friend is to be one.*
—Ralph Waldo Emerson

*Friendship is like money, easier made than kept.*
—Samuel Butler

Being a friend is about caring and sharing. A friend is respectful and peaceful in relating to others. Being peaceful does not mean that a friend always lets the other person have his or her own way. Instead, the friend learns to deal with situations assertively to make one's own needs known while learning about the needs of the friend. There is a sharing and caring when deciding on a course of action that will hopefully be of benefit to both. In the Bible, Paul the Apostle wrote a famous description of love in his first letter to the Corinthians 13:4-8. James Muriel and Louis Savary adapted these verses to apply to friendship:

> *Friends are patient and kind,*
> *they are not jealous or boastful, they are not arrogant or rude.*
>
> *Friends do not insist on their own way, they are not irritable*
> *or resentful, they do not rejoice in what is wrong, but delight*
> *in what is right.*
>
> *Friendship bears all things, believes all things, hopes all*
> *things, endures all things.*
>
> *Friendship never ends.*

# I Involve Yourself In Efforts To Make A Difference

*I don't know what your destiny will be, but one thing I know: that the only ones among you who will be really happy are those who have sought and found how to serve.*

—Albert Schweitzer

There are many ways to involve yourself to make a difference. Start with parenting and be involved with children to promote their growth in a positive manner. Be involved in the neighborhood to create a positive climate.

Be involved to stop bullying. Obtain a copy of the safe-environment programs from your child's school. The program usually includes ways to stop bullying. Know the rules and policies that affect your children at school. Take any concerns, questions, or suggestions to the administration of the school.

Be a role model by practicing "random acts of kindness." These practices can begin the chain of kindness and replace teasing and bullying. A few examples of practicing random acts of kindness are:

- Write a note of thanks or appreciation to someone who would not be expecting it.
- When going on a walk, pick up the littered trash along the way.
- Engage in a meaningful conversation with a lonely person.
- Laugh out loud and share your mirthful spirit and smiles generously.

*Scatter seeds of kindness everywhere you go.*
*Scatter bits of courtesy, watch them grow and grow.*
*Gather buds of friendship, keep them till full blown.*
*You will find more happiness than you have ever known.*

—Amy R. Raabe

## M  Monitor Exposure To Electronic Media

*The longer we dwell on misfortunes* [and violence], *the greater is their power to harm us.*

—Voltaire

All media significantly affect the way people view their world. While electronic media may enhance one's mirthful spirit, much of the electronic entertainment available today appears cruel, violent, and bawdy. Frequent exposure desensitizes people to such behavior. They may become numb or apathetic when they observe violent or bawdy behavior around them.

Adults need to monitor electronic media programs. Select and allow those which teach the values and virtues which foster responsible and civil behavior. This includes monitoring humorous programs, because humor today is often inappropriate. Just because a program makes one laugh does not mean that it is a good influence on others. One way to monitor these programs is to have the television set and other sources in the family room or another room where it can be heard and observed. Hours of watching can be limited. There are often options available which can block certain programs. When the material is inappropriate, turn it off and discuss the reasons for the inappropriateness with the child. Replace the activity by engaging the child in a more positive activity such as crafts, coloring, games, going for a walk, or reading. Even better give the child a choice in the replacement activity. This teaches the child to make good choices and lessens any power struggles which may occur when denying something. A good rule of thumb is that when taking something away give something desirable in return.

## U  Unite Others In The Efforts

*He can inspire a group only if he himself is filled with confidence and hope of success.*

—Floyd F. Filson

There is strength in numbers. Discussing various approaches for action with neighbors and others may create a unified front and consistency in dealing with some of the concerns which may arise. For example, if a certain television show is not allowed in any of the homes in the neighborhood, the decision may be more acceptable to a child. If consistent bullying is observed in the neighborhood, then it may be helpful if a group of parents take action in an assertive, caring, and respectful manner.

Communities are becoming more progressive in providing positive activities for children. Many schools provide child care for working parents. These programs usually include structured activities, and some even include opportunities to do homework. Many community centers offer a variety of wholesome activities. Parent-teacher organizations may jointly sponsor fun activities for the whole family.

## L Live In The Way That You Teach; Be A Role Model

*Example is not the main thing in influencing others, it is the only thing.*

—Albert Schweitzer

*A good example is the best sermon.*

—Benjamin Franklin

The best way to teach others is to be a role model. Children learn by imitating the behavior of those around them. For example, many abusers come from abusive homes. Breaking the cycle of violence is very difficult. It may require reporting the abuse to a professional who can provide intervention.

While one may not be able to change the behavior of others, one can change the way one reacts to the behavior. This can teach children more acceptable ways of responding to another's unacceptable behavior. Being a good role model also means acting in a caring, respectful way so children will learn positive values by example. To be sure that the role modeling is observed and greeted in a positive, learning manner, it also helps to talk about the behavior and discuss the situation.

## I  Instill A Mirthful Spirit

*All times are beautiful for those who maintain joy within them; but there is no happy or favorable time for those with disconsolate or orphaned souls.*

—Rosalie Castro

Instilling a mirthful spirit in yourself and in others will help promote a joyful life. The joy and fun that a bully may feel from bullying is different from the inner joy and fun associated with a mirthful spirit. A mirthful spirit is optimistic, hopeful, peaceful, and calm, not destructive, corrosive, abusive, violent, or stormy.

Television KARE 11 of Minneapolis, MN uses a slogan from the acronym B-U-L-L-Y to summarize a way that the stimuli can be changed. It stands for **B**uilding **U**nderstanding, **L**ove, and **L**earning for **Y**outh. Changing the stimuli which leads to bullying is not easy, but it is possible. Create opportunities to do good. Help children help themselves. Apply zero-tolerance rules in a thoughtful manner. Nurture empathy. Give lots of appropriate hugs, smiles, and good humor. Enhance self-esteem. Support children in making choices. Teach friendship skills. Make a difference. Monitor exposure to electronic media. Unite others for action. Be a role model. Instill a mirthful spirit. Make these your guidelines to help create a caring, non-violent environment. Maintaining a mirthful spirit has a role in preventing the trail from teasing to taunting to tragedy.

*Never doubt that a small group of citizens can change the world. Indeed it is the only thing that ever has.*

—Margaret Mead

# Growing and Aging Mirthfully

*You grow up the day you have your first
laugh at yourself.*

—Ethel Barrymore

As we age, we develop physically, socially, psychologically, and so on. Our senses of humor also develop as we age. Humor is age-specific, so appreciate it and laugh along. When you understand this normal growth and development, you become better able to cultivate humor, mirth, and laughter throughout your life and the lives of others. Efforts to nurture smiling, healthy humor, and laughter must begin in infancy and continue throughout life.

## Babies

*There is no cure for birth or death save
to enjoy the interval.*

—George Santayana

A baby's smile is a heart-warming, perhaps life-changing moment. The smile tells you the infant is satisfied and content. Smiling is also one of the few options in an infant's limited array of non-verbal communication choices. Nurturing parents and caregivers bond with infants by encouraging them to smile and giggle with gentle tickling, peek-a-boo, patty-cake, and other silly games. Babble with babies, be silly with them, talk with them, and make eye contact when doing so. Bonding builds esteem, trust, security, and a sense of delight. With loving verbal and non-verbal techniques and games, one can nurture laughter and contentment in infants and help them anticipate mirth and joy. If you need some assistance there are books to help, such as *97 Ways to Make a Baby Laugh* by Jack Moore.

# Toddlers And Preschoolers

*From there to here, from here to there,*
*funny things are everywhere.*

—Dr. Seuss

Children at this age may laugh as many as 400 times per day. Amazing! Since parents may not find all 400 occasions appropriate or becoming, a crucial dilemma arises: How to discipline wayward behavior yet not punish or stifle the laughter that often accompanies such behavior. Said differently, parents often discipline children in ways which the kids understand as instructions not to laugh. We've all heard these comments: *What's so funny? Wipe that smile off your face. This is not funny.*

Our suggestions for fostering humor, laughter, and mirth with this age group correspond precisely with broader parenting tactics. Rather than constantly exercising your power and control over children by incessantly telling them "no," try to distract, divert, and redirect your child away from wayward behavior toward acceptable behavior. Remind children about being gentle, kind, and caring. This tactic is not easier or quicker than saying "no," but it is more effective in the long run. With this challenge in mind, remember that a parent may need to take a deep breath before reacting to a child. The parent may need to walk away for a few moments to compose himself or herself. Consider your choices before over-reacting. And remember that no matter what, you are setting an example for the child, modeling behavior that the child will conclude as "reasonable" and expected.

With children at this age, parents must anticipate conflict, tension, and power struggles over toilet training, "forbidden behaviors," and public versus private behavior. Forbidden behaviors include any behavior — such as bodily noises, nose picking, swear words, and such — that parents try to curtail, especially in public. Public and private issues arise when a child asks, for example, why she can kick a ball at the park, but not in the living room; why she can splash at the pool, but not in the tub; why she can read and talk aloud at home, but not at the library or at church. Try to find and express humor in these often awkward moments. A lighthearted touch will save you much aggravation and reward you with a mirthful spirit. And remember that words like "poopy-head" are very funny to toddlers. Get used to it. Divert. Distract. Chuckle under your breath.

*Laughter is the natural sound of childhood.*
—Alvin Schwartz

## Grade Schoolers

*If you lose your power to laugh,*
*you lose your power to think.*
—Diane Benton, First Grade Teacher of
Adam Goodman in *Laffirmations*

Children this age continue to find forbidden behaviors funny. Respond with appropriate balance and calm. By age six kids also enjoy riddles and knock-knock jokes.

> *Knock, knock.*
> *Who's there?*
> *Ima.*
> *Ima who?*
> *Ima tired of knocking. Let me in.*

> *What kind of fish purrs?*
> *A catfish.*

By age eight kids also enjoy puns and short, funny stories. *Jokes for Children* and *More Jokes for Children* (Kohl and Young, 1966 and 1984) offer many examples:

> *How much is five Q plus five Q?*
> *Ten Q.*
> *You're welcome.*

Children eight to ten years old enjoy slapstick humor and physical comedy, such as a person slipping on a banana peel or getting unexpectedly doused by a water hose.

> *What is worse than finding a worm in your apple?*
> *Finding only half a worm.*

Such humor often involves a "victim." Again, a dilemma arises: How to encourage humor and levity without injuring or victimizing others.

In this context the problem of teasing arises. It is normal for children to want to feel good about themselves, and one measure of "goodness" is to be better or superior to others. Teasing becomes an obvious strategy. Yet such teasing easily provokes retaliatory, escalating rounds of teasing. Further, at this age, children begin to notice features or characteristics of other children that may seem "unusual" or abnormal. We all know the hit list of physical, social, and personal traits.

If the child being teased becomes sad or angry, he or she will likely be accused by the teaser of being unable to "take a joke," a further source of teasing. *Are you a crybaby? What a wimp.* If uninterrupted, such negative humor may come to dominate teasers' senses of humor and victims' senses of self-esteem. Some people never grow out of put-down humor. And some people never escape the dark shadows of the put-downs. We probably know someone who has heard jokes all his life about his weight, stutter, teeth, or such.

Indeed, some people develop a deep, painful fear of being laughed at. Some simply flee. In the extreme, some people actually freeze—their muscles strongly contract, their minds close down or go blank as a defense reaction—when laughed at or shamed. Henri Bergson (1956) and Michael Titze and Waleed Salameh (1996) call this frozen reaction the Pinocchio Complex: A person's movements become stiff and wooden; the face becomes mask-like.

When children are unable to develop a sense of belonging during their growing-up years, they often feel clumsy, awkward, and insecure with groups of people. They can never quite relax. One reason for this behavior emerges in the family life of the youngster, particularly in the child's relationship to his or her mother. Self-centered, unhappy, stiff mothers often raise children who become insecure and un-relaxed.

## KEY POINT

We firmly, deeply believe that only positive humor that avoids injuring or victimizing others can promote mirth and wellness. Teasing, taunting, and laughing AT others may be funny to some, but it will not promote wellness in our view.

*A good laugh is sunshine in a house.*

—William Thackeray

## Teens

*Every kid should have a joke-a-day to keep the glums away.*

—Ann Bishop

Adolescence can be painful and awkward as teens worry about peer acceptance, physical changes, sexuality, "fitting in," popularity, and so on. Teens ask themselves: *Who am I? What makes me special? How do I fit in? Who cares about me?* Some teens enjoy what analysts call macabre or ghastly humor: extreme behavior, amusement at violence, practical jokes, humiliation of others, and in-group jokes at the expense of "out-groups." For some, "out-groups" might be parents, teachers, awkward teens, the vulnerable, and so on. Practical jokes are often orchestrated by a group. Efforts to have a good time "at the edge," but not be embarrassed by or in front of parents and the opposite sex, are central concerns.

Unfortunately, alcohol and drugs often accompany efforts to behave in extremes and become associated with "having a good time." This confusion between humor and a good time can lead to addictions and distorted behavior. Parents must be wary. Research by Mary Huntley reveals that many people fondly recall the laughter, play time, and warmth of family gatherings during their youth. Perhaps a warm, attentive, mirthful family deters drug and alcohol abuse.

Adolescents in their mid- to late-teens often begin to develop a more mature sense of humor that veers from laughing at people to creating humor. Kidding often replaces teasing. Such teens become more interested in telling jokes and stories amusingly, with attention to timing, wording, and skill. Such teens are also better able to understand abstractions, double meanings, subtlety, nuances, and the humor of ideas rather than physical conditions.

A successful, enjoyable adolescence is a foundation for life. Teens wrestle with and "try on" various identities and ways to package their identity through hair styles, clothing, music, language, habits, and so on. Conversations with teens often reveal their enjoyment at living uniquely and provoking responses.

*When the going gets tough, the smart get…laughing.*

—Joel Goodman

# Adults

*Laughter has no age. It belongs to all generations—
especially when it's shared. That's the secret of crossing the
generation gap.*

—Bob Talbert

Society often sends the message that humor and fun are the habits of
youth. As adults we must "grow up, get serious, get a job, and go to work."
No wonder teens want to delay the responsibilities of adulthood as long as
possible and prolong apparent fun.

It turns out that the healthiest and most productive worksites value a
light and humorous atmosphere. We prize a sense of humor in the people
we date and marry. Humor allows partners to endure and overcome the
challenges of marriage and the tribulations of parenthood. Parents who
play with their children, who enjoy the art and passion of playfulness, will
foster laughter in their lives and in the lives of others. The tasks of parenting and marriage become easier when one learns to laugh with children
and spouse.

Shirley K. Trout, in *Light Dances: Illuminating Families with Laughter
and Love*, offers page after page of wonderful counsel to parents about
saturating your lives and homes with humor and laughter. She declares
that the intentional use of humor and laughter helps children learn, creates positive memories, fosters family harmony, and promotes positive,
healthy relationships in other aspects of children's lives. Create games, use
dramatic gestures, make up silly words and songs, be playful. Children
will pay attention, become engaged, feel better about the situation, and
focus on the issue at hand. Why wrestle or struggle with your child over
bedtime, homework, chores, curfew, and the like, when you can laugh and
play? Humor outweighs scolding and iron-fisted discipline when helping
children conform to expectations.

*Jest…in case you're wondering what you want to be when you grow up.*

—Joel Goodman

Middle-aged adults often work too much, creating imbalances in their lives. Levity and humor often take a back seat to responsibilities. Do you know anyone who whispered on her deathbed that she wished she'd spent more time at the office? Balance is crucial. Humor promotes balance. Adults with an upbeat sense of humor are more resilient, healthier, more supportive partners, and strengthened for the adversities of life. As Abraham Lincoln said so memorably, "People are about as happy as they make up their minds to be."

## Older Adults

*Laugh while you can. There is nothing more biodegradable than happiness.*

—Mary Durham

Older adults experience loss of abilities, family members, and friends. If they can avoid losing their sense of humor, they cope with aging more successfully. The ability to laugh at one's self and at aging creates a healthy attitude toward aging. The motivational speaker Karen Kaiser Clark has collected a list of comments that older adults find amusing.

> *Everything hurts, and what doesn't hurt doesn't work.*
> *The gleam in your eyes is the sun hitting your bifocals.*
> *Your knees buckle, but your belt won't.*
> *Your mind makes contracts your body can't keep.*

A doctor told Leona, an 86-year-old, that even modern-day medicine cannot treat all concerns. "I can't make you any younger," the doctor said. Leona replied, "I don't want you to make me any younger. I want you to be sure I get older."

Be fully present for the people you engage. Share memories with caring, compassion, and smiling eye contact. You will foster mirth, health, and happiness.

*When I die and anyone thinks about it, rather than a moment of silence, I'd much prefer a moment of laughter.*
—Bob Talbert

The development of humor runs a specific course. We foster humor, laughter, and mirth first through eye contact with infants, then through amusement at forbidden behavior, then by laughing at wittiness. Then we lose our humor in the reverse order. Elderly people may lose their ability to understand the incongruity or inconsistency that underlies much wittiness. Then they often find forbidden behaviors less amusing. Yet we never lose our appreciation and desire for eye contact and smiles and their ability to spark amusement, pleasantness, warmth, and personal connection, even among those suffering from dementia. Using humor to engage the "twinkle in one's eye," according to Kaye Herth, will likely create desired connections, especially among the elderly.

Another way to think about growing and aging mirthfully is to use the acronym B-R-I-D-G-E. The growth and development pattern of humor, mirth, and laughter is linked like a bridge spanning one's life. Remembering what we need to do at each stage to promote growing and aging mirthfully is presented by each letter of the acronym.

**B** *Babble with babies*
*Be silly, coo, babble, and enjoy the smiles and little giggles that tickle our hearts when we see and hear these satisfying human responses from the wee ones.*

**R** *Rejoice and redirect*
*Rejoice in the laughter expressed by toddlers and pre-school children. When they begin to say their own funny witticisms, laugh even though they may not make sense. Redirect the child when humor is used to hurt other people and pets.*

**I** *Invite a "laughing-with" attitude*
*During the grade school ages, invite children to laugh WITH others and un-invite laughing AT others. This promotes healthful use of humor, mirth, and laughter rather than harmful use.*

**D** *Develop "laughing-at-self"*
*Teen-age years provide opportunity for developing the ability to enjoy goof-ups and embarrassing moments made by oneself and allowing others to laugh along with you. Those who have developed a good sense of self-esteem and self-confidence will be in a good place for this step.*

**G** *Giggle and guffaw with gusto*
*Even though life may be serious during adulthood, use or create opportunities to laugh with gusto and enjoy as many belly laughs as possible. Allowing the urge to giggle and guffaw with gusto provides a whole body exercise that has the potential to promote health and prevent illness for the rest of your life.*

**E** *Eye contact and enjoying human connections*
*During advancing years, human contact with smiles and pleasantness afford the best mirthful responses. Eye contact, enjoying pleasant memories, and easing up on jokes will have positive results for the majority of older adults.*

*You don't stop laughing because you grow old.*
*You grow old because you stop laughing.*
—Michael Pritchard

*When you come to a fork in the road, take it.*
—Yogi Berra

# Poetic Musing:
## Resolutions For Your Mirthful Spirit

Because today is the first day of the rest of my life on this earth,
I will enhance my life through these resolutions on laughter
and mirth.

I will attempt to maintain a mirthful spirit every minute.
I will not let a day go by without seeking some laughter in it.

I will look for laughter in everyday happenings and absurdities.
I will use laughter to cope, survive, and grow in the midst of
adversities.

I will use humor only in a positive, playful, and loving way,
While looking at the bright side of events that occur during
the day.

I will expect laughter to enhance my physical vitality,
While also serving as a stimulant to my sociability.

I will maintain my mirthful spirit by releasing my "elf."
As I go through life I'll remember the best source of laughter is
myself!

# PART III
Focusing a
Mirthful Spirit
in the
Work Place

# Employing Mirth in All Kinds of Work

*There is work that is work and there is play that is play.*
*There is play that is work and work that is play.*
*In only the last lies happiness.*

—Gelett Burgess

Lydia is a wonderful example of a lady who maintained a mirthful spirit and made work fun wherever she went, despite many adversities during her life. She grew up in Germany during World War II. As a teenager, she worked in an underground munitions plant in Kreiburg, near Munich. She skipped work one day to have a picnic with a male friend, a German soldier, on a wooded hillside overlooking the munitions plant. She watched in horror as U.S. bombers flew over the site at noon and bombed the plant. No one inside came out alive. Lydia says, "Don't tell me it doesn't pay to play hooky. If I hadn't skipped work that day, I wouldn't be alive today."

In 1948 as a "German war bride," she came to America when she was 22 years old, with very little money and knowing very little English. Most of her jobs in America were as an assembly line worker. She and her coworkers have many mirthful experiences to recall. When working at a Birdseye packing plant, corn was packaged on the second floor. On the last day of the corn pack, it became a tradition for Lydia and several of her co-workers to slide down the banister to the first floor, celebrating the end of the pack. She said the managers often greeted them and said with smiles on their faces, "Don't you girls ever grow up?"

While working at a Munsingwear plant stitching men's shorts, she said the company gave her a new sewing machine to use one day. A manager did a time study to see how fast she could sew with the new machine. Although she was paid by the pieces she completed, she was afraid to set a new higher standard for herself, so she sewed at a leisurely pace. The manager said, "Lydia, you can sew faster than that." Lydia responded, "Just because you put a new engine in the machine doesn't mean you put a new engine in me." The quota was established and within two days following the new sewing machine, Lydia doubled her quota. Those who knew her well just shrugged and said, "That's Lydia!" She made the working environment fun, yet was always productive and efficient.

What lesson can we draw from Lydia's lightness, buoyancy, and humor? The best lesson is that mirthfulness leads to productivity. The acronym P-R-O-D-U-C-T-I-V-I-T-Y is used to describe the benefits of mirth at work, and the acronym M-I-R-T-H-F-U-L-N-E-S-S gives suggestions for maintaining a mirthful spirit at work.

**P**  *Polishes the company's image*

**R**  *Relieves tension*

**O**  *Optimizes team morale*

**D**  *Decreases resistance to change*

**U**  *Unleashes creativity*

**C**  *Cuts absenteeism and costs*

**T**  *Tames conflicts*

**I**  *Increases effectiveness*

**V**  *Vitalizes communication*

**I**  *Increases cohesiveness*

**T**  *Triggers self-confidence*

**Y**  *Yields profits*

## P   Polishes The Company's Image

*Mirth is a presence in the world, like the sun,*
*that shines on everybody.*

—Edna Thayer

We are sure you have noticed the difference between companies which radiate a mirthful spirit and those with serious or even grumpy employees. We prefer to do business in companies where smiles abound. The smiles radiate to others like the sun's rays and polish the whole image of the company.

## R   Relieves Tension

*Congenial labor is the secret of happiness.*

—Arthur Christopher Benson

Humor provides a comic relief from everyday stress. It gives a mental and physical break to clear the mind and relax the body.

## O   Optimizes Team Morale

*Pleasure is reciprocal.*
*No one feels it who does not at the same time give it.*

—Lord Chesterfield

Terry Paulson, Ph.D., writes in *Making Humor Work,* "A benefit on any job is laughter. It should never be a crime to have fun on the job; it may very well be a crime not to have fun. And best of all, it doesn't cost a penny." Making a work setting enjoyable increases morale, cooperation, and rapport.

## D   Decreases Resistance To Change

*Only a baby likes change, and even they cry sometimes.*

—Source Unknown

In the fifth century B.C., Heraclites said, "The only constant is change." Change is the biggest stressor on the job and the speed of change keeps increasing. Change is inevitable. It has been said that when one rests, one rusts. No wonder some people feel as if they are on a treadmill that will not stop. While one cannot stop change, a mirthful spirit helps control actions, reactions, and attitudes toward change.

## U   Unleashes Creativity

*Happiness lies in the joy of achievement and the thrill of creative effort.*

—Franklin Delano Roosevelt

Humor relaxes, eases tension, and clears the mind to allow room for creativity. Alertness, playfulness, and relaxation coexist in the open frame of mind. Because humor enhances creativity, humor can promote innovations for change. Creative thinkers play with ideas, risk foolishness, and become more effective in problem-solving.

## C   Cuts Absenteeism And Costs

*In the Orient, people believed that the basis of all disease was unhappiness. Thus, to make a person happy was to restore him to health.*

—Donald Law

When a job is fun, people want to come to work. A mirthful spirit at work increases attendance and decreases the costs associated with absenteeism.

## T   Tames Conflicts

*When you can't solve the problem, manage it.*
—Robert H. Schuller

*The art of living lies less in eliminating our troubles than in growing with them.*
—Bernard M. Baruch

Anger and conflict can be disarmed with humor. Breaking the tension caused by anger and conflict sets the stage for solving the problem and managing the conflict. Rather than trying to do away with conflict, it is better to manage it to provide learning and growth situations and work benefits for the company. Laughter is just as contagious as negativity. Having a positive attitude is the first step in managing conflicts. When hit with angry comments, sometimes a witty response will disarm the anger and release the tension. It needs to be done in a way that does not put the other person down. For example, when someone is really yelling, perhaps the response could be, "Thanks, I needed that." The next step is to learn the real cause of the conflict. Behind each person's angry attack is a problem that needs to be resolved by using positive problem-solving techniques.

There are no hopeless situations, only people who think hopelessly. Treating conflict as a challenge is a stimulus for making things better.

## I   Increases Effectiveness

*The only way to be effective in my job is to have a sense of humor.*
—Harry S Truman

Here's an example from sales where the use of humor increases effectiveness. Because humor builds rapport, it lays the groundwork for providing a dialogue as equals. The rapport that is established creates a bond between the seller and potential buyer. Humor allows the salesman to be entertaining and inspiring while informing. A salesperson might use humor by putting a note on the outside of a letter which says, "Please open before reading." If a customer comes in to complain asking, "Who's the idiot in charge?" the response might be, "I'm the head idiot, what can I do for you?" Think of the mirthfulness if someone who says, "no," to a sales pitch is thanked with the comment, "I need five "no's" for every "yes." Do you know someone else who will say, "no" so I can get closer to a "yes"?"

## V   Vitalizes Communication

*Joyful words are vehicles that can transport us from the drab sands to the dazzling stars.*

—M. Robert Syme

Communications are more fun to read when the dazzle of humor is added. Using clip art, cartoons, or carefully selected sayings increase the odds that the communication will be read or heard. One worker who sends many fax messages created a cover sheet which was headed, "Little Known Fax," and includes statements such as "Every minute in the United States, 590 boxes of Jell-O are sold." A CEO stapled Kleenex to a memo which contained an unpleasant announcement about downsizing.

## I   Increases Cohesiveness

*Laughter is a glue that helps people stick together.*

—Edna Thayer

Nothing builds rapport faster than humor. The rapport that is established creates a bond which leads to cohesiveness in working toward personal and company goals. Consider the 2005 season for the Minnesota Vikings, an NFL football team. After seven games, the team's record was two wins and five losses. Then the starting quarterback was severely injured and the reserve quarterback began to lead the team. Disaster loomed. Yet the Vikings won six in a row. The reserve quarterback had a light, infectious attitude. He grinned and encouraged his teammates to have fun. An Associated Press article in the Sports section of the *Free Press* published in Mankato, Minnesota, on December 14, 2005, attributes the success to a change in the atmosphere within the locker room.

> *Six weeks ago it was a cold and tense atmosphere. The primary interactions between the players consisted of mean-spirited jokes and sharp jabs at each other. Success has been the perfect elixir. Now the laughter stems from good-natured humor. One player said, "Everybody was just straight honest with each other. We just started to pull together."*

## T   Triggers Self-confidence

*Happiness hates the timid!*

—Eugene O'Neill

As the world looks on, a smile and a mirthful spirit trigger others to have good thoughts. This promotes one to believe in one's ability, power, and judgment.

## Y   Yields Profits

*We live in an ascending scale of benefits when we live happily.*

—Robert Louis Stevenson

Instead of being viewed as "goofing off," humor in the work place yields profits. A mirthful spirit in the work place often increases attendance which decreases the costs associated with absenteeism. Sick time may be cut along with medical costs. Sales and production levels may increase.

Yes, I want to be cheerful and happy at work. How do I do that? The acronym M-I-R-T-H-F-U-L-N-E-S-S gives suggestions for both the employee and the employer.

**M** *Maintain a collection of humor from the job*

**I** *Include humorous objects in the work place*

**R** *Rebut detrimental humor*

**T** *Take time for yourself*

**H** *Honor co-workers*

**F** *Find ways to give joyful surprises*

**U** *Use ice-breakers and attention-getters*

**L** *Live mirthfully*

**N** *Nurture the positive; neutralize the negative*

**E** *Enhance communications with mirth*

**S** *Savor special moments*

**S** *Schedule stress breaks*

## M   Maintain A Collection Of Humor From The Job

*Seize from every moment its unique novelty and joy.*

—André Gide

Collect humor associated with the job. Maintain a humor file. Jot down those situations which have proven to be a source for joyfulness. These could be kept in an album or scrapbook to be shared with everyone, or posted in a mutually accessible place for the employees. Be sure the list does not include things which would offend others. Poking fun at oneself is acceptable. In fact, being able to laugh at and share examples of one's errors and sources of embarrassment help others learn to do the same.

## I  Include Humorous Motivational Posters At Work

*The greatest happiness in the world is to make others happy.*

—Luther Burbank

Create sources of fun at work by decorating the environment. Display motivational posters. Examples are:

- Your attitude determines your altitude.

- Any person who says it cannot be done should not interrupt those who are doing it.

- There are three kinds of people: those who make things happen; those who watch things happen; and those who are unaware of what happened.

## R  Rebut Detrimental Humor

*Different men seek happiness in different ways.*

—Aristotle

It goes without saying that caution needs to be taken when using humor at work. Chapter Six describes detrimental humor which should never be used at work. Humor must not offend anyone. While humor may not work with everyone most of us enjoy a mirthful spirit.

## T  Take Time For Yourself

*Happiness depends upon ourselves.*

—Aristotle

Scheduling times of fun, rest, and relaxation is just as essential as scheduling daily activities of life. One needs to purposefully include whatever it is that adds mirth to one's life. Some experts say that a person needs thirty minutes each day just for self. Self-renewal activities are personal and individually selected. Do whatever renews your spirit: soak in a tub, read a book, meditate, listen to music, reflect on the positive happenings of the day.

## H   Honor Co-workers

*I know well that happiness is in little things.*

—John Ruskin

Expressions of appreciation, verbally or in writing, are one way to honor co-workers. One manager of 175 people made it a point to compliment each employee at least once every six months. This could be verbally or through a written certificate of appreciation. A record was "secretly" kept to be sure no one was missed. Also, the first-line supervisors were given classes on coaching employees and were encouraged to give their workers praise and encouragement while helping them achieve their goals.

## F   Find Ways To Give Joyful Surprises

*Pleasure is the object, duty, and the goal of all rational creatures.*

—Voltaire

We like fun surprises. We bet you do, too. Find ways to give joyful surprises to people in your work place. It might be bringing a special treat to share at break. We know a place where the management gave each employee a birthday card on the birthday and an anniversary card on the anniversary of the date of employment. These cards can be inexpensively created on the computer.

Joyful surprises may also happen by scattering fun objects in the work place. There are many commercial items available which can evoke a laugh when activated, such as a flower pot of artificial sunflowers which plays, "You Are My Sunshine." In addition, objects such as koosh balls, play dough, or similar items may be placed on a table to provide levity during a meeting.

## U  Use Ice Breakers and Attention Getters

*Humor unlocks the listener's ability to be receptive to what is being said.*

—Mary Huntley

Humor serves as a great way to break the ice and grab attention at meetings and during conversations. A simple idea for a small group is to bring an assortment of caps and hats, and ask each one to put on a thinking cap. When everyone looks around at each one wearing a hat, people are perceived differently and the mood becomes lighter.

Another idea of a mirthful way to open a problem-solving meeting: Use a magic light bulb (purchased from a magic store) that lights up when the end of the bulb is touched by metal foil. Keep the small square of foil on the inside of the palm of one hand. Then invite participants to come up with bright ideas of ways to solve the problem or conflict—ideas bright enough to light up the light bulb—while touching the bulb being held in one hand to the hidden foil in the other hand to produce light. After ideas are generated, be sure to select some for action and then follow through. Give appreciation for the idea along with the reasons why some ideas were not selected.

## L  Live Mirthfully

*Act as if you were already happy and that will tend to make you happy.*

—Dale Carnegie

We cannot create happiness and spread it to others unless we first have it within ourselves to spread. Maintaining a mirthful spirit requires planning and actions. In his book *Act Now,* Dale Anderson describes a research study which shows that we feel how we act. If we go around discouraged, pessimistic, and depressed, soon that is how we will feel. However, if we act happy, optimistic, and mirthful, soon we will feel that way even if that was not how we began. Life always contains both positive and negative experiences, both happy and sad. We need both the sunshine and rain in life. Keep smiling when the rain comes and it will brighten the day.

## N Nurture The Positive; Neutralize The Negative

*It is an optimistic man who can enjoy the scenery while taking a detour.*

—Dian Ritter

A popular song from the 1950s contains lyrics which encourage people to concentrate on the positive and do away with the negative while focusing on the affirmative. Most situations have both a negative side and a positive side. Our attitude helps determine which one we choose for our focus. We can often change our outlook as well as that of those around us by focusing on the positive side of a situation instead of the negative.

## E Enhance Communications With Mirth

*Give me a man who joyfully sings at his work.*

—Thomas Carlyle

Creative humor enhances communication. For over 12 years, an assistant administrator of a rural hospital included a newsletter with the payroll checks, which were distributed every two weeks. The newsletter was limited to one typewritten page on both sides. It contained the latest news from work, the list of employees (with their consent) having birthdays during that two weeks, good news to share about employees, and other items of interest. The newsletter started with a motivational saying, and ended with something humorous or thoughtful. Typically, graphic art, stickers, or some mirthful attention-grabber was added. Imagine her surprise on retirement when she realized some people not only read but also collected these letters from all 12 years.

Some jobs require giving speeches. Does the tree that falls to the ground in the middle of a huge forest with no one around make a sound? Of course it does, but there is no one to hear it. The same is true with many speeches. Unless one is successful at gaining the listener's attention no one will hear the excellent information presented. An effective talk is not only informative but it is also entertaining and inspiring.

Ministers belong to an occupation which requires many speeches or sermons. In his 2003 dissertation, Douglas Damron reports that humorous sermons are found to be more persuasive. Congregations appreciate a minister who knows the art of appropriately interjecting humor in the message. Joel Osteen from the New Lakewood Church in Houston, Texas, is an example of a preacher who starts each televised message with something funny. On February 12, 2006, his humorous beginning was:

> *A woman was surprised in her home by a burglar.*
> *Not knowing what to do, she quickly shouted, "Acts 2:38!"*
> *The burglar fled but was later apprehended by the police.*
> *The police were curious and asked the burglar why he fled.*
> *The burglar replied, "She said she had an ax and two 38's."*

## S  Savor Special Moments

*Now and then it's good to pause in our pursuit of*
*happiness and just be happy.*

—*The Cockle Bur,* Anonymous Author

Take time to smell the flowers; take time to savor the special moments. Mirthful moments happen spontaneously. Be receptive and open. Face life with a positive attitude. When the special moments happen, take time to acknowledge and experience them.

## S  Schedule Stress Breaks

*If we could learn how to balance rest against effort,
calmness against strain, quiet against turmoil, we would
assure ourselves of joy in living.*

—Josephine Rathbone

Schedule stress breaks. Companies are doing such things as going to a "casual Friday" when less business-like attire can be worn. Employees may be encouraged to contribute a "joke of the week" which is then displayed in a prominent place. Placing a humorous prop in the break room will add to the lightheartedness. Some companies host fun events for their employees, being careful to include families when possible so as not to infringe on family time. If the company is not providing for adequate stress breaks, provide your own within the parameters of the job.

Balancing a serious job with mirth and laughter is tricky business. A job needs to be taken seriously and work needs to get done. Mirth and laughter need to remain with the person doing the job, not with the job itself. Humor must not interfere with the work or the accomplishment of goals. Since people can have markedly different senses of humor, workplace humor must be appropriate and inoffensive.

Huntley's 1988 research study shows that when people are focused on a project, interrupting with humor could be unwelcome and unappreciated. Thus, timing your humor and respecting people's need for focused work is critical and important.

A mirthful spirit and smiling are useful in all work environments. Specific examples of using humor in the work setting for health-care workers and for educators follow in the next two chapters. If you are not employed in health care or education, you may want to skip ahead to Chapter Twelve.

*There is nothing better for a man than to enjoy his work.*

—Ecclesiastes 3:22

# Using Mirth in Health Care

*Always laugh when you can. It is cheap medicine.*
—Lord Byron

Humor therapy is an alternative medicine which offers many benefits for those who are receptive. Such therapy has its place alongside massage, therapeutic touch, music therapy, art therapy, aroma therapy and the like. It is a vital component of a holistic health practice. While humor therapy is not necessarily a cure for a disease, it can alter one's response to illness and thereby facilitate healing. Humor can also prevent certain diseases, especially stress-related illnesses such as heart disease, stroke, cancer, and depression.

On June 1, 2000 the Association for Applied and Therapeutic Humor adopted the following definition of *therapeutic humor:*

> *Any intervention that promotes health and wellness by stimulating a playful discovery, expression or appreciation of the absurdity or incongruity of life's situations. This intervention may enhance health or be used as a complementary treatment of illness to facilitate healing or coping, whether physical, emotional, cognitive, social, or spiritual.*

Health-care workers can realize the benefits of a mirthful spirit in three distinct ways: caring for people, sharing with colleagues, and caring for self.

# Caring For People

*When we love and laugh with our patient, we elevate the highest degree of healing, which is inner peace.*

—Leslie Gibson

A humor assessment is the first step in using humor therapy. It forms a blueprint for actions. While at the College of Nursing at Northern Illinois University, Kaye Herth developed in 1984 a copyrighted "Funny Bone History" which can be used as an assessment related to humor. She recommends that an assessment include five main areas: values/beliefs, appropriateness, timing, receptiveness, and responsiveness. The Funny Bone History consists of eleven questions:

- *When was the last time you had a good laugh?*
- *What kinds of things make you laugh?*
- *How often do you laugh?*
- *How do you feel when you laugh?*
- *What role did humor play in your family while growing up?*
- *Imagine yourself as a comedian/comedienne. Who would you be and why?*
- *When was the last time you played?*
- *What could you do today that would make you laugh?*
- *If you put more play and laughter in your life, how would you feel?*
- *Do you find humor a source of relaxation?*
- *Each time you laugh in the next week, write down what made you laugh.*

Recognizing that a thorough patient assessment is very lengthy, perhaps one would not have the time to ask eleven questions related to humor. The inclusion of a single question, "What brings you joy?" or "What makes you joyful?" would be a step in the right direction. It would begin the personal inventory process for the patient and be a stimulus to recall pleasant thoughts and memories.

The responses to the questions will give clues suggesting ways in which a health-care worker might plan actions which incorporate the use of mirth and laughter. The patient could be assisted in purposefully planning activities which lead to a mirthful spirit. In her role as a family nurse practitioner Herth not only used the assessment tool with patients, but also she was among the first to actually write a prescription for laughter.

There are many documented stories in which patients credit the use of laughter, mirth, and a positive attitude in aiding the recovery process. Perhaps one of the best known is the testimony of Norman Cousins. He was a writer and editor for *The Saturday Review* with no background in medicine or nursing. In 1964 he was hospitalized with a severe, chronic, and painful arthritic-like condition known as ankylosing spondylitis. He found that viewing funny videos, such as *Candid Camera, Groucho Marx*, and *The Three Stooges*, would give him up to two hours of pain-free relaxation. He said that he checked out of the hospital into a hotel where he could laugh twice as hard for half the money. He researched the benefits of humor and learned that people feel better when they laugh because of the release of endorphins, which are the body's own naturally produced morphine-like chemical and act by reducing physiological and psychological pain.

Norman Cousins became a pioneer in extolling the virtues of the use of humor and a positive attitude to promote wellness. Before writing his book he wrote magazine articles, and, in 1978, he accepted a position as a lay person on the medical faculty as an adjunct professor at UCLA Medical School, where he established a Humor Task Force to coordinate and support clinical research related to humor.

Health-care facilities developed various strategies to apply the benefits of humor in their settings. One hospice unit at St. Joseph's Hospital in Houston, Texas, developed a "Living Room" which contained various ways to tickle the funny bone, such as cartoons, videos, books, posters, tangible objects, piano, and more. Patients could choose whatever they wished that looked interesting to them. Duke University developed one of the most comprehensive facilities where patients could select from a wide variety of art, music, literature, and laughter stimuli. Other humorous nursing interventions have included a scrapbook of cartoons; collections of humorous sayings, buttons, or bumper stickers; or keeping a journal of things that bring mirth. Dentist offices began putting positive and clever posters on their ceilings to attract the attention of their reclined patients. Some volunteer groups took a humor cart from room to room from which, depending on the infection control considerations of the unit, patients could select or purchase items of cheer. Clowns began to visit patients, especially in pediatric units. Humorous videos were offered as a choice on closed-circuit television. Dr. Patch Adams developed an entire health-care complex, the Gesundheit Institute in Hillsboro, West Virginia, utilizing the benefits of humor in the healing process.

Health-care workers who give medicine know the five rights of administering a medication. Equally important are the five rights of using humor therapeutically. These are: right time, right place, right amount, right relationship, and right rapport. Prior to using humor therapy, consider the patient's age, values, culture, anxiety level, physical condition, level of pain, and medication. Humor needs to be used with empathy, sensitivity, warmth, and caring. Sometimes a patient's laughter in certain situations may actually be a seeking of more information or conversation. Listen for cues beyond the laughter.

Tickle therapy is an example of a specific use of laughing for therapy. Harry Zehnwirth, a pediatrician from Australia, describes a six-year-old girl with cystic fibrosis who received tickle therapy twice a day from her mother. Tickling is an engaging and effective way to carry out chest physiotherapy. Vigorous laughter from gentle tickling is almost always followed by a good productive cough. The mother had intuitively found that tickling her daughter was a good way to help her cough. C. W. Metcalf states that infants respond positively to tickling from the mother or a trusted adult, but respond fearfully to tickling from strangers.

## KEY POINT

Positive humor occurs between people who know each other and have a trusting relationship, with implied permission for play, fun, laughter, and jokes. The same type of humor between strangers may have a negative effect.

Humor therapy has a role in the treatment of clients with chemical abuse patterns. Laughter, along with tears, serves as a catharsis which could serve to rebalance the brain neurochemistry following deficits caused by substance abuse, withdrawal, or excessive seriousness. Tears actually contain some of the toxins associated with stress and can be useful in eliminating them from the body. A chemical-dependency treatment unit in southern Minnesota provided a series of classes called, "Positive Addictions." The topics included good nutrition, exercise, relaxation, sleep and rest, support groups, and laughter. All of these have the potential to increase the body's endorphins and provide a natural way of feeling good without reaching for the outside chemical.

Humor may not be appropriate with certain mental states, such as confusion, depression, paranoia, schizophrenia, obsessive-compulsive behavior, hysteria, or during the height of a crisis. Humor at these times may be misunderstood and interpreted in a threatening way or uncaring manner. Appreciation of humor by the patient may actually be a sign of recovering from these states. If humor is to be used in these situations, then it is best left to a skilled therapist.

The inappropriate response to humor may be a symptom of various types of diseases including pseudobulbar palsy, multiple sclerosis, Lou Gehrig's disease, Wilson's disease, epilepsy, Pick's disease, Alzheimer's disease, Kleine-Levin syndrome, schizophrenia, paranoia, hysteria, and the manic phase of bi-polar disease. In these cases laughter may be inappropriate to the stimulus, uncontrollable or unrestrained, forced, compulsive, or overly cynical.

To be successful at humor therapy the health-care worker needs to cultivate a sense of humor and model a mirthful spirit while showing genuine empathy and sensitivity. Contrived cheerfulness and artificially trying to be funny might be resented and actually cause negative effects. Creating a warm, friendly, and reassuring atmosphere and smiling genuinely is the most therapeutic approach. When using humor, it is important to remember that what is appealing to one may be appalling to another. A smile and a mirthful spirit are rarely misunderstood. Proverbs 15:30 says, "A cheerful look brings joy to the heart." Herth states that positive humor connotes kindness and congeniality, carrying a message of affection, caring, and humaneness. The core conditions of caring are warmth, authenticity, and empathy.

**KEY POINT**

Caring helps make the real connections at the heart
which allow for laughing or crying,
depending on one's need at the time.

## Sharing With Colleagues

*Happiness is like honey, when you pass it around some of
it will stick on you.*

—Dian Ritter

The life of a health-care worker can become very stressful when frequently dealing with matters of life and death. Humor is often used as comic relief from the everyday stress. This humor may take on the form of inside jokes or may take on a darker side called "gallows humor." This is a grim humor typically seen when individuals are faced with considerable stress and dangerous situations in their struggles with life and death. Gallows humor is not unique to health-care workers. Law-enforcement officers and military troops use gallows humor, too. The purpose is to use irony or sarcasm as an escape from the psychological stress of reality. Gallows humor allows one to "clear the mind" from the tense situation and return to a normal frame of mind before going on to the next case. It gives a mental break. While gallows humor can provide relief, it must be used cautiously. It can be easily misunderstood as a non-caring attitude, and should never be used around anyone who might overhear and misunderstand.

Using humor in the work setting begins with maintaining a positive attitude and a mirthful spirit. This can be enhanced by posting captions or cartoons in the work setting. One employee bathroom had a large sign which stated, "This is your day. Hope everything comes out okay." Another bathroom had a sign which read, "The job isn't done until the paper work is done," referring to all the required paper work in health care.

Keeping a list of humorous occurrences provides a source of humor. An example from the patient's chart includes: "Patient was discharged alive, without permission."

Using humor during a teaching encounter can help establish rapport. A conversation about the need to lose weight might begin with, "It appears that you are a little too short for your weight." Patients often initiate the humor. One woman tells of being hospitalized for a quadruple by-pass surgery. During the pre-surgical visit by the anesthesiologist, she decided to tell him a joke. She told a fictitious story, stating that on her airplane flight there was a need for an emergency surgical procedure aboard the plane, a tracheotomy for a person who could not breathe. Luckily there was a surgeon aboard the plane. The flight attendant asked on the loud-speaker if there were an anesthesiologist on board. There was one who readily volunteered and went to the section of the plane where the surgery was being done. He asked what he could do to help, and the surgeon said, "Change the light." Because anesthesiologists are often asked by surgeons to change the light for better vision during surgery, a task which certainly does not require all the years of academic preparation needed to give anesthesia, it became a stimulus for hearty laughter. The two established an instant rapport.

During the downsizing and eventual closure of a unit for the developmentally disabled at a state hospital, there was considerable stress and anxiety among the workers. The management initiated a "Rib Tickler" award. Each week co-workers could nominate a colleague who had done something to "tickle the ribs" or bring humor to the work environment. The winner of the weekly award received a rack of ribs. It contributed to a mirthful environment and made it a little easier to accept the inevitable.

Start a problem-solving meeting with something funny. For example, think of mental floss as a curved plastic tube, the diameter of a straw, through which a long small cord has been strung. Placing the tube behind the head from ear to ear and pulling the cord from side to side gives the impression that the cord is running through the head from ear to ear. Then say, "Today anyone who needs to is encouraged to use this mental floss to get rid of the old ideas and ways of doing things and make room for newer creative ideas." Another idea is to put on rubber gloves to inspect the problem. Short ice-breakers at the start of the meeting generate laughter, relieve the mind from tension, relax the group, and pave the way for creative thinking.

Sharing a mirthful spirit is a great way of keeping the mirthful spirit. It has the old boomerang effect. The Scottish poem, "A Bit of Sunshine," says it all. John Wallace Crawford uses this poem to convey the message that when one has sunshine or laughter it should be thrown to a person who is feeling blue. As soon as one throws it, the laughter and sunshine will come back as a boomerang to the person who shared the feelings of mirth and laughter.

# Caring For Self

*The person who laughs, lasts.*

—Mary Poole

"Physician, heal thyself," is an expression which has been used to make the point that in order to effectively care for others, one must first care for oneself. This expression is equally true for all workers in health care. We strongly believe in the importance of caring for self and advise you to revisit Chapters Five and Nine for helpful hints in maintaining a mirthful spirit.

*Humor is a spark igniting the positive energies needed for healing.*

—Research Participant

# 11

# Applying Mirth in Education

*Pleasant words are like a honeycomb, sweetness to the soul
and health to the body.*

—Proverbs 16:24

The classroom setting benefits greatly from a mirthful atmosphere. In her 2002 dissertation, Kathryn Manning reaffirmed earlier beliefs that appropriate humor in middle school classrooms may be used to "reduce stress, master difficult information, develop higher-order thinking skills, and de-escalate tense situations." The chemical catecholamine, which is released through laughter, increases alertness, enhances short-term memory, and promotes creativity. The acronym E-D-U-C-A-T-E describes major benefits.

**E**  *Enhances short-term memory*

**D**  *Diffuses tension*

**U**  *Unleashes creativity*

**C**  *Cuts absenteeism*

**A**  *Accelerates alertness and attracts attention*

**T**  *Triggers motivation for learning*

**E**  *Enriches learning environment*

## E   Enhances Short-term Memory

One of the effects of the catecholamine chemical which is released in the bloodstream by laughter is to enhance short-term memory. This will help the student who is learning new facts and concepts. Repetition in recalling these facts will then help commit the information to long-term memory.

## D   Diffuses Tension

Laughter and humor diffuse tension between people. Edna's husband used humor often at school to diffuse tension. One example happened at Faribault Junior High School in Minnesota during a physical education class. The locker rooms were located in the basement, a floor below the gymnasium. Obviously, he could not be in both places at the same time. One day as he went from the lockers to the gym, he saw two junior high boys ready to square off and fight each other. Being quick-witted, he walked over to the boys, tossed them a volley ball, and said, "No, no, no–dancing is next week; today we play volley ball." The boys began to laugh, the tension was broken, and the boys joined in the fun of the class. Humor can be an acceptable outlet for aggression and release hostility and anger. While it does not "cure" these underlying feelings, it does serve as a diversion to get to the task at hand.

Some years later Edna's husband became an assistant principal at the junior high. He never remembered to water plants in his office, so he bought an artificial tree. He decided he would place an artificial bird on the branch of the tree. The bird chirped on motion. When students were sent to him for disciplinary problems, they would brush the branch of the tree when entering the room and the bird would start chirping. It would be just enough lightheartedness to break the tension, facilitating discussion of the concern of the moment.

Use of humor just prior to a test can help relax the students and provide for better test results. Appropriate use of humor can decrease anxieties such as those associated with achievement. It can help establish trust between the teacher and students. One college teacher did an exercise where the students gave themselves a head massage prior to taking a test. Watching the others massage their heads provided levity for relaxation.

## U  Unleashes Creativity

A mirthful spirit and laughter have the potential of unleashing creativity through the same catecholamine which enhances short-term memory. Removing stress and tension from one's mind can free the mind to pave the way for the brain cells to be more flexible and make new connections. Creativity is a useful component for learning, as it can lead to problem-solving. A mirthful environment in the classroom increases creativity.

## C  Cuts Absenteeism

If the learning environment is fun, children will more eagerly anticipate going to school and will be less tempted to skip school or think of ways not to attend. When humor and laughter promote wellness, there will be less illness and fewer days missed because of sickness.

## A  Accelerates Alertness And Attracts Attention

The catecholamine chemical increases alertness. Being alert is helpful in the learning environment. Many of the educators who were interviewed during our research study state that they often used humor as an attention-getter in class. They describe the importance of getting the attention of students before attempting to teach. This could be accomplished by starting the class with something humorous.

## T  Triggers Motivation For Learning

A positive, mirthful environment increases motivation for learning. Children at any age want to be part of a situation that is fun. Keeping attitudes positive can build rapport, improve morale, and foster team spirit, which enhance learning. Negative attitudes, such as scolding, harsh and strict enforcement of rules, and an environment that is too rigid and serious, can demoralize a group and lead to difficulties in the classroom.

## E   Enriches Learning Environment

The best environment for learning is one where tension promotes curiosity and a desire to learn, where creativity and raising questions is promoted, where people want to spend time, and where people feel good about themselves and what is happening. We believe this environment includes the classroom, playground, lunchroom, bathroom, media center, and all academic rooms. Humor helps create a caring and trusting environment where learners need not be perfect and mistakes are tolerated, fostering student participation and learning. There is an accepting and caring milieu where there is freedom to explore and try new options and increase critical thinking skills. Communication is enhanced in this non-threatening environment, and there is an exchange of ideas and questions which promote group cohesiveness and problem-solving.

# Creating A Fun Learning Environment

*A day ought to start with eager anticipation
and end with pleasant memories.*

—Dian Ritter

Attend any high school class reunion and one of the most frequent topics of conversation centers around favorite (and possibly not-so-favorite) teachers. Alumni are quick to extol the virtues of their favorite teachers. One of the single most important criteria for being in the favorite teacher category is making learning fun. Here are ten ways to create a fun learning environment.

1.   Get to know the students. Know what things they enjoy doing.

2.   Purposefully include mirthful, fun activities in the lesson plan.

Humor strategies do require preparation, time, and creativity to convey a message. It becomes easier with practice. Some use cartoons to bring home a point. Some teachers have created poems or stories to illustrate ideas. Some tell appropriate jokes. Games such as Jeopardy or Trivial Pursuit related to the course content add fun. The humor has to match the content for that day's class lesson. Humor unrelated to the course content may actually distract. Humor which is related may lead to increased retention of the content. One fun way to summarize a chapter from a text book might be to divide the class into groups of four or five, and have them compose a song to a popular melody of their choice, using key concepts from the chapter. The songs are then shared with the rest of the class. It's a great way for students to review the key points of a chapter without listening to a lecture.

Fred Riehm is a retired teacher who taught ninth-grade math and science in West St. Paul for 35 years. He is a master at using puns and quips appropriate to the ongoing conversation. He says that he has had years of practice. He would watch the eyes of his students. When they began to have a distant look, he would throw in a one-liner appropriate to the topic of discussion and bring their attention back to the class. He said it is important to use quips which are related to the content, because using a non-related joke with this age group does not work. An example of a joke related to the content is when he was talking about shapes of lenses, he said there was a man who fell into a lens grinding machine; he made a spectacle of himself. (Pause.) Then he claimed he was framed. Fred uses Jack Benny's belief that the pause and timing are everything. He was asked if he ever thought about writing a book about all of his sayings, and his answer was that he did not want to be in a "bind." He thought people would be "paging" him all the time. He said he no longer drinks coffee because he does not want to have "grounds" for complaints. Besides, when he drank coffee, he used to go "stir crazy." His years of practice have made this mirthful approach to life a part of his delightful personality.

3.  Start the class with something fun or funny.

Humor is a great attention-getter. Perhaps students listen more carefully because they don't want to miss any future jokes, or perhaps it is the catecholamine chemical that is released through humor that increases the alertness and attention. Whatever the reason, many teachers have found the benefits in using humor as a way to attract the attention of students during the class. Once they have the attention, the teacher can go on to talk about the lesson for the day.

4. Use humor as a topic for various activities which are intended to teach a communication skill and social bridging.

One topic for "Show and Tell" in elementary class could be something funny which has happened to the student. In secondary classes humor could be a topic for a speech or a paper. At the college level students might even be able to choose a course on "Humor and the Humanities" to meet a communications course requirement.

5. Capitalize on humorous situations.

Spontaneous situations often occur during a class which can provide a stimulus for humor. When using this approach it is important to only laugh WITH a student, never AT a student. Sometimes the safest source of humor in a classroom is the teacher. Being able to laugh at oneself is a gift. One teacher in a college classroom recalled an event where she was wearing a skirt with a button at the waist. The button gave way. As the skirt was slipping to the floor, she was able to laugh and say, "Now that I have your attention, does anyone have a safety pin?"

6. Give awards and rewards to provide positive experiences.

It may be as simple as drawing a smiley face on a good piece of homework or adding a word like, "Wow," "Great," "Good Work," "Excellent," "Super." Most teachers put the number correct at the top of the page instead of the number wrong and use a more joyful color of ink than red. Even when helpful suggestions are needed, they can be accompanied by saying something positive in addition to the constructive suggestions.

Pat Luehmann, a judge at a 2005 County Fair 4-H demonstration day had a wonderful understanding of this concept. An eight-year-old girl gave a demonstration. Eight-year-olds receive only a participation ribbon, so there was no need to compare this demonstration with the others for evaluation. The grandmother who accompanied this girl knew that the demonstration had been memorized. However, the girl became so nervous during the demonstration that her mind went blank and she read the demonstration, looking down at her cue cards most of the time. When the judge's comments were received, the only check marks were in the "excellent" column for topic, posters, organization, beginning, ending, and clever attention-getter. In the areas which needed improvement, such as eye contact, no check mark was made and only a comment like "could look up more" was made. This little girl was totally thrilled with the experience and ready to try again the next year.

Many people who work with children, such as teachers and coaches, have a readily available supply of stars and stickers. Besides comments referring to excellence, some stickers include phrases like, "Improved," or "Good Try," so that each child may truthfully receive a sticker. Teachers may also include a major activity which the students enjoy at the end of a particularly lengthy project, such as a walk outdoors in a nature area.

7. Create an environment which has a zero-tolerance for teasing and bullying.

All 50 states now require school districts to have safe environment strategies which include a bullying prevention plan. Teasing and bullying are mentioned in the chapter "Finding Mirth During Distress" as one of the detrimental forms of humor. Further discussion appears in Chapter Seven, "Preventing Negative Teasing."

8. Be a role model.

Plato said that true teaching is one achieved by example. Actions speak louder than words. Sometimes actions speak so loudly that people cannot hear what is being said. A teacher who wants to create a fun environment needs first to have a mirthful spirit. Then, and only then, can it be transferred to others in the class. Being a role model can be one of the most effective ways of creating a fun environment.

9. Avoid the pitfalls of inappropriate humor.

Humor which hurts instead of heals and which leaves people feeling worse instead of better is not appropriate in any setting. This is especially true in the classroom setting, where experiences are so influential in promoting a positive self-esteem for life's challenges.

10. Set the climate to promote mirthfulness and joyfulness with administrative support during teacher-orientation days, and at faculty meetings.

Equally important as the climate within the classroom is the climate between students and administration. There are principals who make it a point to mingle with the students and know most of them by name. Others have made it a practice to greet each student with a smile when students enter the building for class. In addition to enhancing learning for students, a mirthful climate can also diminish burn-out and enhance job satisfaction and performance among the teachers.

> *A teacher affects eternity; he* [she] *can never tell where his* [her] *influences stop.*
>
> —Henry Adams

# Poetic Musing:
## Resolutions For Mirthfulness At Work

I will be mirthful at work, and use laughter in a respectable way,
While being serious about the goals that need to be accomplished that day.

I will refrain from using humor that would potentially offend,
And if it accidentally happens, I will make sincerest amends.

If others use teasing and laughter that might be demeaning to me,
I will smile and not be offended, thinking "they didn't mean it to be."

If I use inappropriate humor, it will be with mutual consent,
With friends who take it and give it back in the good-natured spirit that's meant.

Once again, I will maintain my mirthful spirit by releasing my "elf."
As I go through life I'll remember the best source of laughter is myself!

# PART IV

## Exploring Laughter Seriously

# 12
## Pondering Historical and Cultural Highlights

*Love may make the world go 'round, but laughter keeps us from getting dizzy.*

—Donald Zochert

Laughter touches every aspect of people's lives. Many scholars on the topic provide rich discussions of laughter that we don't often think about. When noting the historical stories related to laughter we can feel very fortunate that civilization has progressed favorably. As the world becomes smaller, so to speak—due to the ease in travel, business exchanges, electronic technology, educational opportunities, and tourist attractions—the need and desire to understand differences in the characteristics of laughter among cultures is helpful.

## Laughter Forever—Change Over Time

*When humor goes, there goes civilization.*

—Erma Bombeck

*Laughter is a powerful tool in a powerless situation.*

—Allen Klein

Laughter has changed over time. An historical review of laughter is rather bewildering, even appalling at times. Wickberg (1997) suggests that a comprehensive written history of laughter is nonexistent. According to him, understandings of laughter have been condensed over the years to theoretical labels. Rather than giving the meaning of laughter and its relationships to the social fabric of the people, we are left with part of the story.

Early reports of behavior note that people laughed whenever they encountered something allegedly inferior to themselves. We call this *ridicule*. Thus, the laughter associated with someone else's mistakes, and slapstick comedy as seen today, have their roots in historical human existence. This form of laughter was traced through history in terms of cruelty of humans to other humans. Laughing AT people seemingly insane or otherwise different and making up nicknames to taunt others are examples of ridicule and derisive laughter. Fortunately moral teachings have helped to reduce these forms of laughter in society today.

From Plato's perspective, people laughed because of their ignorance, so were people in powerless positions. From his way of thinking, amusement caused loss of control. Therefore, leaders and authorities must avoid laughing. The best model of a person was one who avoided the urge to laugh. This may be where the idea of seriousness at work had its origins. Changing those ideas has taken a long time. We continue to work at it, as suggested in Part III.

During the time of medieval monarchies, the court jester was a recognized necessity. Conrad Hyers explains the jester's role was to stimulate laughter in the king. The jester used himself as the target for ridicule and whatever else would stimulate humor and laughter. Keeping the king happy helped protect others from potentially harmful punishment. Today, comedians, clowns, mimes, and circus performers have become a part of entertainment for all in society. They invite us to laugh with them and to express our enjoyment of their skill and antics.

People often say that something was so funny they almost died laughing. One can imagine someone laughing and laughing because something triggered enormous amounts of laughing for several minutes. These are times when people feel like they can hardly catch a breath before feeling the impulse to laugh more. There were times reported in historical events when punishment was given to people on the one hand while providing humor for audiences on the other hand. People were held in a captive position, tickled incessantly such that a person was not allowed to take a breath. The ultimate consequence was suffocation or bursting of a blood vessel and death. This is one reference to laughter causing death. Today, we would not have a similar situation with such severe consequences. When one is being tickled, the "victim" often requests that the pursuer stop. Today, tickling is usually done in a playful way and the extreme situation fortunately does not occur. However, the reference to "gentle tickling" is stated as such for a good reason. "To die laughing" is then a figure of speech indicating an extreme case of being triggered to laugh heartily.

Writings by Donald Hayworth in 1928 and Charles Gruner in 1978 provide explanations from their respective complex studies. The notion of laughter communicating a sense of safety was described by Hayworth. Gruner suggested that it may be impossible to determine if laughter had a beginning, since humans have always had the capacity to laugh. It is known, however, that humans laughed before they had a language and, thus, before jokes existed. Since Gruner supported the "sudden glory" theory of laughter, or what Morreall referred to as an emotional shift, he believed that laughter originated in the beginning of time when man's roar of triumph was portrayed as winning in aggressive fights for people's survival. This laughter is visible today in a variety of ways, such as when an athletic team wins and realizes its sudden glory. The team members cannot hold back their smiles and jumps for joy.

Another interesting historical perspective is one in which the types of humor have changed over time. Vera Robinson, nurse educator emeritus from Fullerton, California, provided a wealth of information about how the comic stimuli have changed through the years. It changes with the social and political climates. Humor stimuli are very individualistic; they are also very generational. What was funny to one generation of people will probably not be as funny to another generation, as the context or the environment contributing to making something funny changes. In fact, it may be said that something that is funny during one era may even be an embarrassment in another era. The ridicule of people seen during the sixteenth to eighteenth centuries would be embarrassing to people in the twenty-first century.

American humor has changed during the course of history. As the country developed, the topics of humor evolved as well, from references to the first settlers, to the migration westward, and development of the Midwestern and Western frontiers. Charting new territory was often fearsome, shocking, and exhausting. Humor depicted the exaggerated experience of the people in order to provide tension relief. Writings by Mark Twain and James Thurber continue to be remembered and enjoyed today.

Robinson elaborated on the Roaring Twenties and early 1930s, referred to as the *Golden Age of Humor,* with memorable characters such as Charlie Chaplin, Laurel and Hardy, the Marx Brothers, Will Rogers, W.C. Fields, and the Three Stooges. Comedy by Red Skelton, Clifton Webb, Buster Keaton, Jack Benny, and Bob Hope were also among the famous. Lucille Ball and Desi Arnaz, Dean Martin and Jerry Lewis were among the favorite comedy teams of the 1940s and 1950s. Jackie Gleason, Art Carney, George Burns, and Gracie Allen were also popular in the post-World War II era. One of George Burns' popular lines was, "You can't help getting older…but you can help getting old." Lily Tomlin, Carol Burnett, and Bill Cosby continue to be among comedy favorites for a variety of ages in today's audiences.

*Comedy has to be truth.*
*You take the truth and you put a little curlicue*
*at the end.*

—Sid Caesar

We admit these comedy stars are among our favorites. However, we learned that our research participants also regarded this group of comedy experts as examples of good, uplifting, and healthful humor. In contrast, many of today's comedy entertainers use more derogatory humor that can be harmful to others. As we have proclaimed loudly and clearly, harmful humor does not lead to wellness.

*Humor is not a trick, not jokes. Humor is a presence in*
*the world—like grace—and shines on everybody.*

—Garrison Keillor

During times of war and political unrest, insecurity among people made both laughing at others and laughing with others difficult. These became times when people felt able to reflect and laugh at themselves. A so-called "new age of humor" emerged in the 1970s, a "renaissance of laughter" as Robinson called it. This reawakening of laughter, with its value, purpose, and importance in life being readdressed, may explain the resurgence of increased interest and writing about humor and laughter. The connections between laughter and health became more and more deliberately tied together in both the popular literature and the professional literature.

*There are three elements in the world—God, Human Folly, and Laughter. And since the first two pass all comprehension, we must do what we can with the third.*

—John F. Kennedy

Varying perspectives describe the comediennes and comedians of today. Comedy Clubs are popular in larger cities. Late-night television talk shows with Jay Leno, David Letterman, and Conan O'Brien continue to be popular. People describe the humor as different because it does not represent the wholesome, generic humor suited for all ages. Rather, one notices more negative humor. People in political and economic positions become the targets of comments intended to be funny. For some, it is a way of reducing tension and making light of the seriousness of political life and governmental challenges. So, is it good or bad? Does it help or hinder your humor perspective? We say, just be careful.

*Jokes are always about things that are wrong. We laugh at our tragedies in order to prevent our suffering.*

—Steve Allen

Shows such as "Raymond," "Are You Smarter Than a Fifth Grader?" "America's Funniest Home Videos," and "The Bill Cosby Show" provide humor entertainment more suitable for families. The sources of humor continue to be all around. There are many options and choices; choose wisely for your own wellness.

*I realize humor isn't for everyone.*
*It's only for people who want to have fun, enjoy life, and feel alive.*

—Anne Wilson Schaef

## Laughter—Cultural Perspectives

*All people smile in the same language.*

—Source Unknown

Laughter is common to all human beings everywhere. However, the stimuli for laughter are quite different because of the living practices unique to particular countries and cultures in the world. In places where there is more freedom of expression, there is more laughter. In places where there is less freedom, fear is more prevalent and the expression of laughter is guarded.

*The freedom of a society varies proportionately with the volume of its laughter.*

—Zero Mostel

The study of humor and laughter related to "culture" surfaces continually whenever a group is gathered to consider the body of knowledge available. The more one begins to study culture and laughter, the more there is to know and discover. One is led to study individual cultures which tend to mirror the heritage of the people where one resides. The individual nature of humor to produce laughter is also individual in relationship to each culture. One needs to understand a specific culture in order to know the ways in which people will recognize incongruity and their laughter will be triggered. Therefore, what may be funny in American culture may be unfunny or unrecognized in another culture. Even in the same country, what is funny in rural America may not be recognized as funny in urban America.

Another dilemma is that the differences across cultures spark humor for a person who lives outside the culture because of perceived differences. In that vein, a laughing-AT response may occur because of the difference noted and without understanding the incongruity from a cultural perspective.

Language translations can often be a source of frustration as well as a source of humor. For example, one time a family of six, consisting of three generations including a nine-year-old girl and a six-year-old boy, was traveling in Norway. The only family member who spoke the Norwegian language fluently was the senior family member, the grandfather. Both of his parents were from Norway and spoke the language during his growing-up years. One day during their travels, the grandfather ordered tickets for a sightseeing tour of the fjords. Speaking in Norwegian, he asked for four adult tickets and two children's tickets. The ticket-booth person asked the ages of the children, and the grandfather reported in Norwegian the numbers "na'n" and "seks." What the grandson noted was a finger pointing to him and hearing the word, "sex." The grandson immediately blurted out in a very serious voice, "I am NOT sexy!" Everyone laughed, with grandpa and the Norwegian woman at the ticket booth laughing the most heartily. The humor was explained to the six-year-old and he also laughed about the altered perception and language interpretation. Just thinking about the incident created smiles and chuckles throughout the remainder of their travels.

At other times language misinterpretations may need to be handled more delicately. For example, being sensitive to laughing WITH versus laughing AT others becomes an important factor to consider during such situations.

One writer, George Goldtrap, believes that cultural differences can magnify situations when people hang onto what is called a "sensitive mood-a-tude." People can miss out on considerable fun and enjoyment if they maintain an inability to accept differences and do not allow a playful attitude about them. When diversity is viewed as not only unique but also precious, the lens people use to see differences changes.

Many humor experts advocate against using "isms" as the brunt of jokes. "Isms" relate to words that end in "ism," such as ageism and racism. The recommendation is that if one is of the same culture, religion, nationality, career choice, political orientation, age, or color of the audience in which such a joke is shared, it is less likely to be offensive. Therefore, if one is Norwegian, one can share Ole and Lena jokes since there is acceptance for laughing WITH rather than laughing AT related to one's own cultural heritage. Likewise, if one is not of Polish descent, it would not be appropriate to tell Polish jokes.

*Laughter has no accent.*

—Jim Boren

Cultural aspects of laughter also relate to the work world. Work places have their own cultures. There are work-oriented languages, spaces designated for certain people and not others, and unwritten expectations that become learned. Part III explores humor, mirth, and laughter in the work place. A work place culture that includes healthful laughter, to us, will be the best. Mirth has its place; check the culture.

Some publications help people lighten up in the serious world of work. *Funny Times: A Monthly Newspaper of Humor, Politics, and Fun* is one of these publications. It includes articles and numerous cartoons and comic strips, some of which we regard as uncouth. On the other hand, to those directly involved with these arenas, the humor is not only mirthful and at times hilarious, it is also therapeutic—another case in point about the fact that humor stimuli are very individualized and not always universally accepted by everyone.

Publications offered four to six times annually that may be of interest to a more general audience are *Laughing Matters,* published in Saratoga Springs, New York, and *Therapeutic Humor, the Newsletter of the Association for Applied and Therapeutic Humor,* published in St. Louis, Missouri. An important consideration is to identify for oneself the sources of humor that create mirthfulness. Laugh everyday and as many times as feels good. On a daily basis incorporate these resources into a life pattern and let them do their work. Many resources for humor and laughter are listed in the Appendices to add awareness to the vast array of choices. Among our most sacred freedoms is the freedom of choice. One's humor preferences for the best mirthful day become a personal choice.

Along with cultural considerations, the relationships of spirituality and religious orientations to laughter may be issues. The perspectives of Conrad Hyers, an ordained minister and professor emeritus of history and religion at Gustavus Adolphus College in St. Peter, Minnesota, and John Morreall, professor of religious studies at the University of South Florida shed some light. Hyers writes that one's religious faith allows the person to have a sense of confidence in God. This confidence provides the person with permission or an ability to feel lighthearted with laughter as an outcome of that experience. People who view their religion with grave seriousness may actually lack faith, because they pursue being right and righteous about religious matters, rather than purporting a faith in God. Thus, such people are more likely to act in a self-righteous manner. The heart of the issue may not be so much about differences in religions as it is about how people perceive their beliefs and religious role.

A pastor in a Lutheran congregation preached one Sunday morning on "being called." Oftentimes people have the sense they have been "called" to do something. For some it is being called to a certain profession, to political life, or to serve others in some way, such as working in Third World countries or leading an action-oriented group. The pastor shared the following humor story about "being called."

One day a farmer was working in his fields. He was an excellent farmer and a Christian man of faith. While on his tractor in the corn field, he looked up in the sky, and in the cloud formations, saw the letters, "G" "P" "C." He interpreted that as a calling for him to "Go Preach Christ." He followed the message and went to the seminary and became a preacher. He was so excited about his first service in a congregation, leading the worship service, and preaching the sermon. However he flopped miserably. His sermon, in particular, did not go well at all. One of the people in the congregation approached him after the service and in a kind and tactful way said, "I think the "G" "P" "C" meant "Go Plant Corn."

Some may interpret this story as a put-down or laughing at someone. However, the timing of the message and saying it directly to the person, and not in front of others, can make a difference in how it is perceived by the other person. It also illustrates the fine line we have mentioned several times earlier.

Cultivating our sense of humor permits the mind to become playful and often triggers insightful creativity and new perspectives. Humor assists the mind by providing some moments of diversion followed by a better ability to problem-solve.

In the name of religion many conflicts have occurred over the years leading to much human suffering. Being open to more perspectives could eliminate these aggressive tensions. Hyers comments that when people can laugh together, the likelihood they will kill each other diminishes greatly. People who laugh together can often listen to one another better, and connections for positive relationships take shape. Engaging the power of positive laughter among people to prevent conflicts and wars would be an amazing achievement. This may be wishful thinking and quite a stretch of the imagination, but why not?

Churches, and all the activities associated with them, have become a wonderful field for sharing good humor. Several books have been published over the years. Two are, *A Funny Thing Happened on the Way to Church* and its sequel, *More Funny Things on the Way to Church*. Pastors and others were invited to share their humor stories, which were then compiled into the books. One true story that happened in one congregation follows:

In several church denominations it is common during the liturgy part of the worship service for the pastor/priest to say, "The Lord be with you." The audience then responds with, "And also with you." One particular Sunday the microphone system was not working very well. The pastor fiddled with the switch, adjusted the swivel part of the microphone, and finally muttered into the microphone disgustedly, "This mike isn't working again." The dutiful audience responded with a booming response, "And also with you."

In the book *Laughter is the Spice of Life*, an anonymous writer humorously shared "Hymns for All Callings" with the following titles:

> *The airline captain's hymn: "Jesus, Savior, Pilot Me"*
>
> *The baker's hymn: "I Need Thee Every Hour"*
>
> *The dentist's hymn: "Crown Him with Many Crowns"*
>
> *The contractor's hymn: "The Church's One Foundation"*
>
> *The boxer's hymn: "Fight the Good Fight"*
>
> *The politician's hymn: "Standing on the Promises"*

*The IRS's hymn: "All to Thee"*

*The dieter's hymn: "And Can It Be That I Should Gain?"*

Bloopers printed in church newsletters or newspapers have become another source of humor associated with the religious community. One example appeared as a headline in the church news section of a local paper: It said, "Come Grown with Us." The mistakes in writing can happen easily and become a great source for chuckles. We hope the person who made the mistake is also able to laugh—a laughing at oneself.

John Morreall shared an interesting piece in an issue of the newsletter of the *American Association of Therapeutic Humor*. He compared Western and Eastern religions and analyzed a common understanding in relationship to humor. In all of the religions people become enlightened by understanding things from the perspective of a higher power. Three things occur: the world takes on a different appearance, people stop worrying about the small stuff, and they become happier. This is also what happens when humor creates laughter. The change that takes place in one's perception causing laughter is also enlightening, potentially even liberating, and creates happiness.

## *Humor is a universal language.*

### —Sid Caesar

The laughing WITH versus the laughing AT perspective is a huge issue that we reinforce repeatedly in this book. Whenever you can assure that laughing WITH is happening, there is safe humor territory. Territory that potentially borders on or invades laughing AT is a more dangerous area. When in such a situation you may want to distance yourself to avoid the temptation to participate in laughing AT. Fostering opportunities to continually help people achieve a comfort level of being able to laugh at themselves at home, at work, at play, and as a member of society is also good advice. Laughter is a wonderful gift. Using it well and respectfully with all people everywhere is the best advice.

*What soap is to the body, laughter is to the soul.*
—Yiddish Proverb

*Laughter is the universal currency of hope.*
—Viktor Frankl

*The most revolutionary act we can commit in our world is to be happy.*
—Hunter (Patch) Adams, M.D.

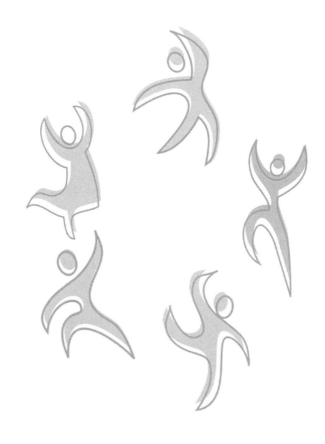

# 13

# Connecting Music and Laughter

*Take time to laugh. It is the music of the soul.*

—From an Old Irish Prayer

A love of music and a love of laughter seem to go together. Some of our research participants specifically pointed our thinking and explorations in this direction. They are accomplished musicians and believe very strongly in the connection. Positive music and positive laughter invoke many of the same qualities in people, which in turn create a mirthful spirit. Attending a mature symphony orchestra, band, or choir concert can be an uplifting experience. People can forget their issues, feel relaxed, and have a sense of joyfulness—a sense of mirthfulness. Laughter experiences often do the same things. After watching a funny movie, people, for that moment in time, will have laid their troubles aside, enjoyed the change in perspective, and will leave the movie feeling relaxed and renewed. A musical comedy provides a combination of music and laughter. The play is often a whimsical one and the musical numbers complement the play with songs and dances. There is a connection between music and laughter—a connection worth pondering.

The language of music contains some words which refer to laughter. The term *music* has its origins in the Greek language and Latin translation. Music means muse. The musing associated with music and with laughter may share similarities as well as differences, but may have the same mirthful outcome. *Vivace* refers to music that is lively and *vivo* directs the musician to play with life. A composition called "humoresque" (French) or "humoreske" (German) suggests that one will hear something of a fanciful, witty nature, or a composition that has a playful or unpredictable quality.

According to Stuart Feder, *scherzo* is an Italian word meaning "joke." It signifies that humor is a major component of the musical number, and the listener should be aware in order to hear it. A similar term, *scherzando*, refers to the sense of playfulness that will be heard in the music piece. The scherzo from Felix Mendelssohn's music for *A Midsummer Night's Dream* is famous. There are many scherzos in music compositions. Even though the term suggests there is a joke to be discovered, they are not so much comical as they are lighthearted.

Franz Joseph Haydn's Symphony No. 94 in G major, the "Surprise Symphony," is well-known for awakening the audience with a surprise, a joke on the audience. The symphony is played softly by the orchestra for quite awhile, then suddenly at the beginning of the second movement a loud chord enters that typically jolts the audience. One can imagine Haydn's delight. Actually, Haydn is well-known for including jokes in his music.

Wolfgang Amadeus Mozart was also a composer who expressed humor, lightheartedness, and mirthfulness through his compositions, such as heard in *The Marriage of Figaro*. Gioacchino Rossini was called the greatest of all Italian comic operas. The music from his composition of the *William Tell Overture* has been used widely. Many of us know the music as the theme song for the Lone Ranger. Johann Strauss, Jr. composed the overture to *Die Fledermaus*. Symphony conductor Dianne Pope shared the story of the famous piece called "Laughing Song," sung by the maid, Adele. In a laughing manner, as operatic singers can do, Adele tries to cover up the fact that she is masquerading as a famous actress at a masked ball. She is actually a maid and the master of the house comments that she reminds him of the maid in his home, which then triggers the song. Aaron Copland and Leonard Bernstein are also well-known composers of music that create enjoyment and a sense of levity.

*The language of all nations is laughter and music.*

—Festival of Languages Web Site

In addition to creating a sense of gaiety, music has also been written and performed to bring a welcome sense of quiet to the listener. "Brahms' Lullaby" by Johannes Brahms has been a favorite of young and old alike for years. Babies have been calmed and lulled to sleep with this melodic and lovely piece. There are other types of music, aside from classical music, which provide soft, soothing, calming, and relaxing slumber. "Twinkle Little Star" can be sung like a lullaby. Some of Yanni's keyboard and instrumental music also promotes relaxation and sleep suitable for all ages. "Enchantment" from his album *In My Time* is a favorite for relaxation. Tami Briggs is a therapeutic harpist who selects compositions and hymns that appeal to various sensory inputs to the brain and promote gradual relaxation, rest, relief from pain, and then sleep. The point here is that peoples' likes and dislikes in music are very individual, just as they are for laughter. Therefore, it is important that one select the music that brings the most comfort or greatest enjoyment.

As children grow, some of their learning experiences are the fun songs that uplift and create playfulness. Many favorite songs come from children's television programs such as *Barney* and *Sesame Street*. Walt Disney-produced films and stories include examples of heart-lifting songs. Action songs have been popular for years, such as "The Itsy Bitsy Spider," "London Bridge," "Old McDonald Had a Farm," "The Farmer in the Dell," "This Old Man," and "The Wheels on the Bus." Adults are amazed at the ability of children to master such songs as "Eddie," where children quickly learn to sing, "Eddie-kucha-kacha-kama-tosa-nara-tosa-noma-sama-kama Wacky Brown" or a song from the Mary Poppins musical, "Supercalifragilisticexpialidocious," or the words that the Fairy Godmother in the Cinderella story sings, "Bibbidi Bobbidi Boo."

*Humor is music to the soul, and you don't have to carry a tune to sing along!*

—John Richardson

Church schools also offer a whole array of fun songs for children to learn that speak of love and happy hearts, such as "If You Are Happy and You Know It, Clap Your Hands." The songs change as the child grows older. However, the playfulness around music continues with the addition of instruments and means of promoting rhythm and harmony. Families enjoy the gatherings at school for which children have spent months preparing their musical programs. Such songs as "Katalina Matalina," "Rocking Roll Body Parts," and "Lettercise" demonstrate learning and fun along with musical joy. The best part is when the parents and grandparents are invited to join in the musical fun. Dr. Jean Feldman's song, "Tooty-Ta," often sung by pre-school children and kindergartners, is an example of a fun action song which concludes with everyone looking very silly and laughing hilariously.

"Kindermusik" is a specially designed program for babies and children through age seven. Parents and their children attend classes, experience music and movement together, and practice together at home. The internationally known program is supported by the beliefs that each child is musical, that parents are the child's most important teachers, and that the child's home is an important place for learning. The program is based on research demonstrating that music nurtures development in cognitive, emotional, social, language, and physical areas. Watching children and parents involved in the program brings the importance of music and mirthful laughter together.

*No symphony orchestra ever played music like a two-year-old girl laughing with her puppy.*
—Bern Williams

As children become old enough to attend various summer camps, more songs are learned. "Blue Jay Song," "Beavers," "Socks Song," and "Moose Song" are some examples. These songs then carry over to school bus rides for field trips. More silly songs emerge such as "Found a Peanut," "I Wish I Were…," "Banana Song," "Princess Pat," and songs sung in rounds, such as "Row, Row, Row Your Boat" and "Are You Sleeping?" This picture of music and laughter continues to unfold along the journey of life. At school dances and wedding dances there are old favorites that continue to delight groups of people as they celebrate together. Examples include the "Hokey Pokey," "Chicken Dance," "Macarena," and the Village People's "YMCA."

High school and college songs sung at athletic events energize people to join in the camaraderie of cheering for the team and enjoying the performance. The mixture of music and laughter is contagious. Team members have often mentioned that the excitement they hear in the crowd at the athletic event energizes their performances, gives them confidence, and fosters positive can-win feelings. The organ music played at ice hockey games or the pep band played for basketball and football games are other examples of giving positive momentum to the sport events.

During times of war, stand-up comedy people and singing groups provide entertainment to the military troops. The combination of laughter and music lifts their spirits, makes them feel special, and is a way of thanking them for their patriotism and commitment to their country while needing to be far away from family and friends doing very serious work.

Adults and some children enjoy the music comedy of Victor Borge. He used his own music talent to invoke laughter at the piano. He played the piano while at the same time offering an entertaining monologue, often with humorous sound effects interspersed and well-timed incongruity. Some may also remember the humorous monologues of the Smothers Brothers. They too combined comedy with music.

There are also made-up songs about laughter to well-known tunes. For example Dr. Dale Anderson (2002) wrote new words to the tune of the "Battle Hymn of the Republic." The words to this song, "Smile," relate to smile, laugh, and grin. The first line of the song is: "It isn't any trouble just to s-m-i-l-e." For the chorus one sings "ha-ha, ha-ha..." By the end of the song, everyone is laughing. Alan Katz and David Catrow created a book released in 2005, *Where Did They Hide My Presents?* It includes well-known traditional Christmas carols with new words they call "silly dilly" Christmas and winter holiday songs. Playfulness and laughter emerge as the familiar music is sung with new words. Fun times are also created in social situations, such as in toasting a person's farewell or congratulating an event by creating new words to familiar tunes. Once again, the combination of music and laughter enhance the benefits each brings to the occasion.

Yodeling is yet another form of music. Many equate yodeling with the Swiss or Austrian Alps and the musical hit, "Sound of Music." Others may relate this unique and rather silly-sounding singing with cowboy days and country-western music. Whenever we hear yodeling, it engages our smiles and represents fun times for people.

The more one thinks about the connections between music and laughter, the more ideas surface to demonstrate the linkages. One could enjoy music in and of itself, and one could enjoy laughter as an entity all its own. However, when both are together there is double the value and pleasure. Opportunities for both are present throughout the journey of life. Being intentional about choices that bring both mirthful music and laughter together creates a powerful potential for embracing health and wellness.

> *The sound of laughter is the most civilized music in the world.*
>
> —Marcia and David Kaplan

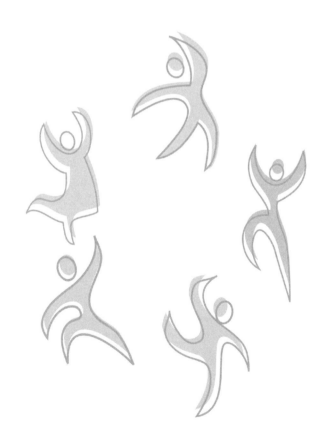

# 14

## ℒearning About Mirthfulness and Wellness

*People with a good sense of humor are part of the greatest show on "mirth."*

—Joel Goodman

How did we learn that mirth, laughter, and wellness are intimately connected? The evidence is everywhere. The research is deep. The conclusions are clear and have been published by many researchers and clinicians over the years. Consider these examples that led our learning about mirth, laughter, and wellness:

- Healthful laughing is a form of physical exercise, aids recovery, strengthens the lungs, and enhances a person's wholeness (Walsh, 1928).

- An important function of laughter is to bring people together for sociability (Coser, 1965; Pattillo and Itano, 2001).

- Laughter has physical, social, and psychological benefits (Robinson, 1970, 1991). Humor heals (Robinson, 1977).

- A good sense of humor improves mental health (McGhee, 1979). Using humor with chronically mentally ill patients is therapeutic (Buxman, 1991). Depressed patients are likely to choose humor rather than non-humor stimuli, even though unable to feel like laughing (Deutsch, 2002).

- Humor and laughter can prevent illness (Goodman, 1983). In his words "Humor can serve as effective mental floss ... a way of promoting mental and physical health."

- Laughter is healthy exercise for just about every organ in the human body (Brody, 1983).

- Humor, mirth, and laughter impact most of the physiologic systems of the body (Fry, 1986).

- "Humor is an antidote to all ills" (Adams, 1992) and a healing agent to problems of people and societies (Adams, 1993). Laughter and health are integrally intertwined (Parse, 1994).

- Therapeutic uses of humor can humanize and strengthen relationships between patients and health-care workers when careful parameters are followed (Berger, Coulehan, and Belling, 2004; Harvey, 1998).

- Laughter can improve immune function, increase pain tolerance, and decrease feelings of distress. Therapeutic effects of laughter have been reported in many clinical areas such as critical care, oncology, hospice (MacDonald, 2004), palliative care units (Dean, 2003), pediatric oncology (Le Vieux, 2002), and among terminally ill patients (Herth, 1990).

- Smiling and laughter on a regular basis, along with socializing, makes life more satisfying and increases a person's happiness (Wallis, 2005).

The study of laughter by many through the years has led to the above understandings and paved the way for further learning in more recent years. Want a quick chuckle? Did you know there are sophisticated names for all of this? Gelotology is a term given to the study of laughter—*gelos* being the Greek word for laughter. Some call such study "humorology." Do you know the original meaning of the word "silly"? Adams (1993) informs us it meant "good, happy, blessed, fortunate, kind, and cheerful in many different languages." Who would ever guess funny could sound that serious?

For even more serious "gelotology," six common theories to explain why people laugh were studied as part of our learning process.

1. People laugh to feel superior to others by laughing at their pain, weakness, or misfortune.

*Superiority theory* is probably the oldest of the theories. Plato, Aristotle, and Hobbes are known theorists. Such laughter is a controlled form of aggression and a self-congratulatory power. People were encouraged to laugh at the deformity of others. In this way those doing the laughing could feel superior. For this reason, Wickberg suggests renaming this "deformity theory" rather than superiority theory. It is basically a form of ridicule and expresses amusement at another's weakness, mistakes, or imperfections. The predominant focus is to laugh at others rather than laugh with them. In today's world, people may want to celebrate by "roasting" someone rather than "toasting." Roasting is laughing AT and toasting is laughing WITH. We recommend "toasting" rather than "roasting" people. Look for the good in people, not the ways to embarrass others without their permission.

2.  People laugh to acknowledge a moment of surprise, incongruity, illogic, or inappropriateness by laughing at the unexpected.

*Incongruity theory* addresses the surprise and amusement one often feels when laughing at something unexpected. An ability to change one's perspective and to see incongruity triggers mirth and laughter. Obtaining a new perspective on something is an important element in being able to see humor for healthful purposes. Aristotle, Kant, and Schopenhauer were noted writers of incongruity theory.

3.  People laugh to relieve tension by laughing at social taboos.

*Release and Relief theory* focuses on the physiological letting go of nervous energy through laughter. What is forbidden or repressed in a culture is often made visible though humor and causes people to laugh. Freud facilitated development of this theory. In terms of knowing there are many benefits of laughing, this theory is regarded as narrow in focus.

A more contemporary version of this theory appears in psychiatrist Christian Hageseth's book, *A Laughing Place.* He advocates an important strategy to use when people are injured or feeling especially tense. When the person feels secure in knowing professional help is on its way, the person is asked to think of a special place—a place where one has memory of feeling relaxed, at peace, and having an enjoyable time. Oftentimes a smile will appear on the person's face, muscles will relax, and the energy needed for responding to healing can occur. The person can focus on the special place rather than on the pain. The notion of a Laughing Place or Happy Place uses mirth to support relaxation and relief of tension. When relaxed in this way, people need less medication for pain, heal more quickly, and seem to get better more effectively.

4. People laugh to refuse to take a situation seriously by laughing at the ludicrous, playful, and overly earnest.

*Play theory* experts believe we laugh when we can no longer take a situation seriously. McGhee extensively studied humor and play. Others claim that no definition of humor is acceptable unless it distinguishes play and seriousness. This view of humor and laughter supports the importance of nurturing healthful expressions of humor and laughter in children. Retaining a playful nature from childhood into adulthood is also important. As some people age, they focus on work and forget about the benefits of play. Winning and success eclipse play, mirth, and fun. Some adults must relearn the art of playing. Playing with children, or playing in childlike ways, reminds us to take time to play and be playful.

5. People laugh to acknowledge the relationship between a lighthearted attitude and a spiritual connection. They laugh to reduce barriers between and among individuals and the Absolute Spirit—whether that be God, Goddess, Allah, Tao, Universe, or Supreme Being.

*Divinity theory* is studied and described by Larry Dossey, a physician and nationally known writer and presenter of holistic health care. He ponders how humor motivates psychological and spiritual growth.

Conrad Hyers offers a Biblical perspective and focus on "divine comedy" (1987). His books and videotapes explore laughter from stories in the Bible. He studied the God-given gift of laughter and wondered why people were so serious about religion and the ways in which religious teachings were practiced. Story after story is lifted from the Bible to illustrate that laughter has a long-standing presence and is intended to be used to promote goodness and loving relationships. As one example, the story of Abraham and Sarah shows how laughter was visible in the Bible. Sarah was an elderly woman, and her husband, Abraham, was 99 years old when they were told they would have a son. Because of their ages, they laughed at the absurdity of this possibility. One might say this was a divine intervention.

When their son was born, they named him Isaac, which in the Hebrew language means "laughter."

*Humor is a prelude to faith and laughter is the beginning of prayer.*
—Reinhold Niebuhr

6. People laugh to express pleasant, unexpected sensations or psychological shifts.

*Psychological Shifts theory* was described by John Morreall in *Taking Laughter Seriously* (1983). He discusses laughter in terms of three psychological shifts: sensory, emotional, and conceptual. Dr. Morreall integrated elements of each of the previous named theories into a more comprehensive theory of laughter, the sixth explanation provided in this discussion.

The notion of psychological shifts explains the peals of delight accompanying peek-a-boo, magic tricks, and roller coasters. Also, we laugh when we are excited, when we reunite with a separated family member or friend, when we win an event, and when we achieve a goal. Further, we often laugh at incongruities that challenge our perceptions and expectations, such as a jack-in-the-box, a tube of springy snakes, and cartoon characters that defy the laws of physics.

*Where there's laughter...there's hope.*
—Comic Relief, 1990

People commonly identify Norman Cousins' 1979 book *Anatomy of an Illness* as opening the doorway to understanding the relationship between laughter and wellness. As introduced in Chapter Ten, Cousins endured a serious, painful illness, and he sought help from his doctor to reduce the amount of medication needed to manage pain. Cousins and his doctor developed a program of high doses of vitamin C and laughter. Cousins viewed amusing movies and television program clips, such as *Candid Camera*. His story is a remarkable case study of how several variables, including positive thinking and laughter, improved his health and disposition. Cousins never declared that laughter causes wellness. He wrote only that it helped him keep a positive outlook and was important to his recovery. However, his experience prompted others to explore the relationship.

In this spirit Huntley extensively interviewed 12 women from 1986 to 1988 on the subjects of laughter and health. The research participants were ages 65 to 83 (median age of 73) and considered themselves well. All were retired university educators, eligible for Medicare benefits, and living in a mid-sized southern United States community. Huntley asked each participant the same set of seven questions.

1. What is laughter?
2. What is the function of laughter in your everyday life?
3. When do you laugh?
4. Explain a time when you did not feel like laughing.
5. Explain the pros and cons, for you, of laughing alone versus laughing with others.
6. Are there times when you purposefully seek out situations in order to laugh? (For questions 1-6, listen for cues which relate any of the above responses to wellness and then pursue or elaborate.)
7. What is wellness?

This lengthy, rigorous, time-consuming process was repeated in 2004 with a different study group that included 20 men and 10 women, each a retired university educator, who considered themselves well, aged 65 to 88 (median age of 73), living in a mid-western community (Huntley, Thayer, and Schuette).

On the basis of these studies we constructed a model of the relationships linking laughter, mirth, and wellness that lead to the conclusions that inform this book. Partial answers to these questions appear as quotations in Chapters One and Two.

We conclude that receptivity to humor in everyday life produces physical delight (smiles to guffaws) and emotional mirth (amusement to pleasure to joy). Such physical delight and emotional mirth jointly contribute to wellness or to what we believe the people described as enjoyable unity. In short, if you are receptive to humor, then you smile or laugh or feel some urgency to respond to the humor stimulus. There is a whole continuum of responses available to people: from smiling to an internal sense of joy or mirthfulness, then to chuckles, and on to gales of laughter. Any of the responses on this continuum promotes wellness.

Some factors inhibit or facilitate one's openness to humor and the amusements of everyday life. However, the sources of humor are unique to individuals and cultures. Nonetheless, even during distress or life's challenges, one can still experience emotional warmth, support, smiles, and mirth. Laughter influences wellness through "vitality and sociability." Laughter begets laughter. It energizes us. It makes life seem fuller and richer. The more one is with others, enjoying laughter and time together, and the more one laughs generally, then the more wellness or enjoyable unity one feels in life.

Further, to the degree one lives with purpose and accepts life's bruises, setbacks, and losses, then the more one experiences life as a harmonious, unified whole. This too is wellness. Our model of these relationships with the circular and feedback representation of the concepts appears below.

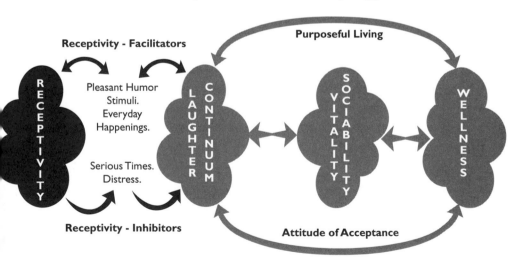

*We now define our terms.*

**Receptivity to Humor** One's acceptance of and openness to seeing or hearing humor. Smiling, mirthfulness, and laughter will not likely occur unless a person is open to receiving pleasant humor stimuli. (Chapters 3, 4, 5, 6, and 8)

**Receptivity Facilitators** Factors that enhance one's acceptance of or openness to humor include pleasant events, ideas, stories, music, along with just being aware of everyday happenings. Humor is everywhere; we just need to notice it—be open or receptive to it. (Chapters 1, 5, 8, and 13)

**Receptivity Inhibitors** Factors that inhibit one's acceptance of or ability to be open to humor include serious times when one needs to focus on a project and distressful times such as: illness; injury; sorrow and loss; tragedy in the world; emotional struggles; sad disappointments; and experiences of ridicule, teasing, and bullying. The more serious the project or more severe the distress, the longer it may take for people to be receptive to humor stimuli. (Chapters 6, 7, and 8)

**Laughter Continuum** A range of physical reactions to humor: smiles to guffaws. A range of emotional reactions to humor: warmth, mirth, pleasantness. Any of these responses leads to wellness at any age. (Chapters 1, 3, 4, and 5)

**Vitality and Sociability** Laughter is infectious and contagious; the more one laughs, the more laughter occurs, thereby creating energy or vitality and bringing people closer together. Vitality represents the many physiological benefits of laughter. Positive laughter creates a bridge for people to bond and to increase their sociability. Social bridging and what we later termed *sociability* represents the psychological and sociological benefits of laughter. All of this affects wellness in a good way. (Chapters 3 and 4)

**Wellness** A chosen, intentional, balanced state of mind, body, and spirit in which a person is able to cope with adverse conditions, experience security and contentment, and express a positive and hopeful attitude about life. Important aspects of wellness are experiencing a sense of harmony and wholeness in life, being at peace with who you are, and functioning in the world pleasantly, meaningfully, and purposefully. Our preferred term is *enjoyable unity*. (Chapter 2)

**Purposeful Living** A feature of wellness that "feeds back" or, in turn, influences a person's openness to humor stimuli. Being able to function in the world and having a sense of peace, purpose, and meaning to life helps a person be more receptive and open to humor stimuli. (Chapter 2)

**Attitude of Acceptance** A feature of wellness that "feeds back" or, in turn, influences a person's openness to humor stimuli. People can have a chronic illness, accept their condition, respond to life situations with laughter, and be well. People also experience other changes during the journey of life, such as disability, loss of loved ones, loss of a job, and any other kinds of losses that cause one to question an ability to cope. Being able to cope, adapt, and move forward is helped with laughter. Developing an attitude of acceptance, and finding a new way to be well, is part of the back and forth cycle from receptivity to laughter to wellness. (Chapter 2)

Our 2004 study confirmed and extended the conclusions of the 1988 research. For example, the recent study underscored the value of social bridging, bonding, and sociability for wellness. It also reinforces the value of extensive, intimate qualitative research, grounded theory, and comparative analysis.

We deeply and passionately learned that people can choose to laugh intentionally, with purpose. We choose to laugh, or not, at risk to our health and wellness. Laughter helps each of us recognize that no one person is the center of the universe. There is nothing that any one person does that is so critically important that one can avoid, ignore, or reject humor. Take time to be playful, to enjoy life, to laugh at your own imperfections. Laugh! It is our prescription for healthful, satisfying living. It is our prescription for embracing and nurturing a mirthful spirit that will foster wellness.

*Laughter is feeling good all over and showing it one place. A smile is a curve that very often can set a lot of things straight.*

—Marcia and David Kaplan

# End Note

*Laughter is a celebration of the human spirit.*
—Sabina White

A mirthful spirit is one of humankind's greatest assets. Laughter has been with us since humans existed. Yet, to recognize the power that laughter has within each of us to make positive differences in the world can often get missed. Learning about laughter from theory, research, history, culture, religion, and music actually emphasizes and supports even more the importance of embracing laughter for wellness. Be open to humor and mirthful feelings—be RECEPTIVE—LAUGH—be WELL.

*Determine to live life with flair and laughter.*
—Maya Angelou

# Poetic Musing:
## Let's Hear It One More Time

Here is our message one more time
Brought to you in this little rhyme.
Be open to humor that's all around.
Opportunities for mirth abound.

Whether you laugh heartily or simply grin,
Healthful benefits you will win.
Rewards include increased vitality
Along with enhanced sociability.

A mirthful spirit will help instill
Purposeful living and a will
To accept challenges that come your way;
Intentionally seek laughter every day.

Enjoyable Unity is the treasure
Your laughter will surely measure.
To a mirthful spirit we truly profess;
Embrace laughter for your wellness.

# APPENDICES

# Mirthful Resources

Resources on the topics of mirth, humor, laughter, and wellness are abundantly available through organizations, newsletters, email addresses, books, web sites, visual media, and catalogs. The resources that we have used or have some knowledge of are included in this listing. We ask you to judge those that pique your interest and those that you want to access on a regular basis. We believe this is part of being intentional about laughter. Deliberately accessing some mirthful and humor-based resources regularly may add a dimension to your life that helps you embrace laughter for wellness.

In this fast-paced century of easy access to information on the computerized Internet, we recommend that you use search engines such as Google or Yahoo. For example, when you enter "laughter" into the search engine on your computer, you may receive over 30 million suggestions. For "humor," it will be even more: 245 million. For "laughter and wellness," the number goes down to 657,000. For "therapeutic clowns," there are 282,000 possibilities. Each of the chapter titles in our book can be entered into a computer search for more information, more than we have chosen to provide for you. The humor, mirth, laughter, and wellness journey becomes endless. You can enjoy designing your own packet of information to supplement what you have learned in our book.

## Organizations, Newsletters, and Periodicals

Allen Klein is known as the Jollytologist. He has written many books associated with laughter including such well-known titles as *The Healing Power of Humor* and *The Courage to Laugh*.
http://www.allenklein.com

Association for Applied and Therapeutic Humor *Humor Connection* is the official publication for members. St. Louis, MO 63105
http://www.AATH.org

American Holistic Health Association (AHHA)
http://www.ahha.org

*Funny Times*, a monthly newspaper of Humor, Politics, and Fun
P.O. Box 18530 Cleveland Heights, OH 44118
http://www.funnytimes.com

International Society for Humor Studies c/o Martin Lampert, Ph.D., Executive Secretary Holy Names University, Oakland, CA 94619
http://www.hnu.edu/ishs

MirthBeat Productions
Minneapolis, MN 55426
Kevin Lee Smith, RNC, FNP, author of a chapter on humor in 1998 book, 3rd Edition, *Complementary/Alternative Therapies in Nursing*, Mariah Snyder and Ruth Lindquist, Eds., Springer Publishing. Kevin Smith is a comic presenter for seminars, conventions, and meetings.
http://www.kevinleesmith.com

The HUMOR Project, Inc.
c/o Dr. Joel Goodman, Founder and Director
480 Broadway, Suite 210
Saratoga Springs, NY 12866
http://www.HumorProject.com

The Laughter-Learning Link Letter
Shirley Trout
P.O. Box 359
Waverly, NE 68462
http://www.teachablemoments.com

## Media and Catalogs on Humor and Laughter

Many companies provide a variety of humor and laughter media resources and seminars. Catalogs announce upcoming presenters to national conferences. All are good resources for locating humor-focused props such as red-sponge noses, smile-on-a-stick, hand clappers, and funny resource books.

Annual Humor Sourcebook
    The HUMOR Project, Inc.
    Saratoga Springs, NY 12866
    http://wwwHumorProject.com

C. W. Metcalf and Associates provide workshops, conferences, videotapes, and books on numerous aspects of humor and laughter. C.W. is a teacher, performer, writer, lecturer, and corporate consultant. He helps people learn and enjoy using humor and laughter to reduce stress.
    Fort Collins, CO 80525
    http://www.cwmetcalf.com

Dr. Annette Goodheart
    Santa Barbara, CA 93103
    http://www.teehee.com

HUMOResources mail-order and on-line bookstore provides a great collection of hilarious and insightful books; videos; DVDs; fun props such as clown noses and smiles-on-a-stick; and MP3 humor teleseminars.
    http://www.HumorProject.com/bookstore

Peter Alsop is a lecturer, humorist, and motivational speaker. He is known nationally as a singer and songwriter using his educational psychology background. He writes songs for children and adults about preventing or overcoming tough issues. Visit his website for more information about his CDs and other recordings.
    http://www.peteralsop.com

Sections of home video and DVD movie stores have a variety of choices for comedy, mirthfulness, and hearty laughter. You can also Google the name of most any well-known comedy people and find a listing of works in paper or media formats. A few are named here to get you started:

Abbott and Costello: *Who's on First?"*

Bill Cosby: *49* A video program about middle-age. Produced by Eastman Kodak, Rochester, NY.

Bill Cosby: *Himself,* 1983.

Victor Borge was a musician and humorist. Some video recordings are:

Victor Borge: The Best of Victor Borge: Act One and Two, New York, NY: GMZProductions

Victor Borge: Birthday Gala, New York. NY: Gurtman and Murtha. 1991.

Victor Borge: Then and Now. Great Neck, NY: CVM. 1992.

Suzy's Zoo has a wonderfully mirthful company of resources for children. Suzy Spafford's animal characters delight children. You can be a member of Suzy's Zoo Fan and Collector Club to stay tuned to her whole line of books, posters, stickers, greeting cards, stationery, and other mirthful items. Two favorite books are listed as examples of her work: *Alphabetical Soup. Witzy and Zoom Zoom.*
Suzy's Zoo, P.O. Box 81266 San Diego, CA 92139
http://www.suzyszoo.com

# More Web Sites

http://www.acthappy.com Dale Anderson, M.D. is a retired family practice physician, board-certified surgeon, board-certified emergency physician, and Minnesota native. His popular books and seminars advocate "healthy, happy INNERtainment."

http://www.afunnybusiness.ca Carole Fawcett describes her stress-management and laughter-therapy workshops.

http://www.bewellderly.com MaryAnn "Annie" Glasgow, founder and director of the Wellderly Foundation, is a psychotherapist and professional speaker. Annie provides a new way of viewing "age" and uses humor delightfully to move from "achieving" to "being."

http://www.bellylaughday.com January 24 at 1:24 PM is the day and time for everyone everywhere to have a big belly laugh.

http://www.comedycures.org A non-profit organization that brings joy, laughter, and therapeutic humor programs to children and adults living with such life challenges as physical illness, depression, and trauma.

http://www.HappyNews.com Byron Reese, an Austin, TX entrepreneur, has several people on his staff who search the news in order to report upbeat and uplifting stories that make people feel good—it is happy news.

http://www.healingpassages.com Ann Weeks is a national motivational speaker on the topics of humor and laughter. She is retired from her roles as nurse educator and nurse family therapist.

http://www.healthypeople.gov/Behealthy Information about the project, goals, and objectives of the Healthy People 2010 initiative are provided.

http://www.humorlinks.com Over 7500 humor links are provided in 560 categories.

http://www.HumorProject.com The HUMOR Project is the first organization in the world to focus full-time on the positive power of humor. Since 1977, they have sponsored 51 international conferences and seminars; done presentations through their Speakers Bureau for more than two million people in the United States, Canada, and abroad; operated the mail-order and on-line bookstore of HUMOResources; been featured in more than 4000 television and radio shows, newspapers, and magazines in over 150 countries; and provided grants to many non-profit organizations to help them tap the positive power of humor.

http://www.ipnrc.org The Parish Nursing Organization focuses on holistic caring, including mirthfulness and spirituality.

http://www.laughteryoga.org Dr. Madan Kataria is the world founder of the international laughter yoga (Hasya Yoga) movement. He and his wife train laughter yoga leaders. Having started in India, there are over 5000 laughter clubs in 40 countries. He aspires to promote this global movement for health, joy, and world peace through training others.

http://www.isd77.K12.mn.us/music/k12music This is a fascinating site for all kinds and types of music for children from kindergarten through grade 12. There is also a link to learn about the 1970s Baby Boomer Bus songs.

http://www.jesthealth.com Patty Wooten has created a web site describing her clown character and laughter information.

http://www.laughterRemedy.com Paul McGhee, humor and laughter expert, provides information on laughter as good medicine.

http://www.laughtertherapy.com Enda Junkins provides a website for advocating the use of belly laughter in relationships.

http://www.laughterworks.com A former stand-up comedian Jim Pelley, provides seminars on how to use humor effectively in the workplace to "smarten up" and enlighten everyday life. One topic is "Mirth Management."

http://www.mirthfulspirit.com Mary Huntley and Edna Thayer created this website to describe their book and how to request copies and presentations.

http://www.natural-humor-medicine.com Clifford Kuhn's book, *The Fun Factor*, is cited through this web site.

http://www.niehs.nih.gov/kids/music.htm This is a delightful resource citing appropriate music for children. There are categories of songs and opportunities to find them alphabetically with a Sing-Along Index. The National Institutes of Environmental Health Sciences includes this because "music is good for you" and it is part of creating a healthful environment.

http://www.nursingfun.com Resources for jokes, games, and travel opportunities for nurses are provided.

http://www.nursinghumor.com Numerous jokes are categorized.

http://www.ofspirit.com Read the story of Margaret McCathie's recovery from severe depression by finding her inner spirit and ability to laugh through connections with Laughter Clubs and Dr. Patch Adams. Google "Margaret McCathie" and click on the article, *The Healing Power of Laughter.*

http://www.RxLaughter.org The healing power of comedy is described. Founded in 1998 by Sherry Dunay Hilber, this nonprofit organization researches and implements projects dedicated to the healing power of comedy during painful medical procedures. Closed circuit television broadcasts the humor. The project began with children and is expanding to adult populations in a variety of care-delivery places.

http://www.successunlimited.co.uk/books Learn more from this web site on how people are working for a bully-free world. A related web site is sponsored by the Field Foundation and author Tim Field, who writes about bullying: http://www.thefieldfoundation.org

http://www.gocomics.com Billed as "the best comics site in the universe," it is a place to test your own creativity with humor and laughter.

http://www.wholeperson.com Books, seminars, and media on stress and wellness are suggested.

http://www.witcity.com A listing of humor related topics, including games for children, gag gifts, and comedy is available.

http://www.worldlaughtertour.com Steve Wilson is cofounder of the World Laughter Tour. He believes that "together we lead the world to health, happiness, and peace through laughter."

http://www.yodelcourse.com Here is a source to learn about yodeling and expert yodelers.

*Enjoy Learning More About*
*Embracing Laughter for Wellness*

# Bibliography

Adams, Patch with Maureen Mylander. *Gesundheit! Bringing Good Health to You, the Medical System, and Society through Physician Service, Complementary Therapies, Humor and Joy.* Rochester, VT: Inner Traditions. 1993.

Adams, Patch. "Good Health is a Laughing Matter." *Caring,* pp. 16-20. December 1992.

Allen, Linda J. "Miracles Happen in Funny Ways." *Therapeutic Humor,* 13(3), pp. 1-2. St. Louis, MO: American Association for Therapeutic Humor. 1999.

Anderson, Dale L. *Never Act Your Age.* Edina, MN: Beaver's Pond Press. 2002.

Anderson, Dale L. *Act Now.* Minneapolis, MN: Chronimed Publishing. 1995.

Anderson, Dave and Tim Wilcox. *More Funny Things on the Way to Church.* St. Louis, MO: Concordia Publishing House. 1983.

Berger, Jeffrey, Jack Coulehan, and Catherine Belling. "Humor in the Physician-Patient Encounter." *Archives of Internal Medicine,* 164(8), pp. 825-830. 2004.

Bergson, Henri. "Laughter." In Wylie Sypher (ed.). *Comedy.* Garden City, NY: Doubleday Anchor. 1956.

Berk, Lee. "The Laughter-immune Connection: New Discoveries." *Humor and Health Journal,* 5(5), pp.1-5. 1996.

Berk, Lee S., Stanley A Tan, William F. Fry, Barbara J. Napier, J.W Lee, L.W. Hubbard, J. E. Lewis, and W. C. Eby. "Neuroendocrine and Stress Hormone Changes During Mirthful Laughter." *American Journal of Medical Science,* pp. 298, 390-396. 1989.

Berra, Yogi. *The Yogi Book: I Really Didn't Say Everything I Said.* New York, NY: Workman Publishing. 1998

Briggs, Tami. "Therapeutic Music to Facilitate Healing, Transformational Growth, and Well-being." *Musical Reflections.* http://www.musicalreflections.com (accessed June 2006).

Brody, R. "Anatomy of a Laugh." *American Health*, pp. 43-47. November/December 1983.

Buxman, Karyn. "Humor in Therapy for the Mentally Ill." *Journal of Psychosocial Nursing*, 29(12), pp. 15-18. 1991.

Buxman, Karyn, Anne LeMoine, (eds.) *Nursing Perspectives on Humor.* Staten Island, NY: Power Publications. 1995.

Canfield, Jack, Mark Victor Hansen, Nancy Mitchell-Autio, LeAnn Thieman. *Chicken Soup for the Nurse's Soul.* Deerfield Beach, FL: Health Communications, Inc. 2001.

Centers for Disease Control and Prevention, National Center for Injury Prevention and Control. Fact Sheets. Available from URL: www.cdc.gov/ncipc/factsheets/yvfacts (accessed July 23, 2006).

Clairmont, Patsy, Barbara Johnson, Nicole Johnson, Marilyn Meberg, Luci Swindoll, Sheila Walsh, Thelma Wells. *Laughter is the Spice of Life.* Nashville, TN: W. Publishing Group. 2004.

Clark, Carolyn Chambers (ed.). *Health Promotion in Communities: Holistic and Wellness Approaches.* New York, NY: Springer Publishing. 2002.

Clark, Carolyn Chambers. *Integrating Complementary Health Procedures into Practice.* New York, NY: Springer Publishing. 2000.

Clark, Carolyn Chambers. *Wellness Nursing: Concepts, Theory, Research, and Practice.* New York, NY: Springer Publishing, 1986

Clark, Karen Kaiser. *How to Know You're Growing Older.* Partial listing from a workshop handout anonymously prepared. Apple Valley, MN: Author. 1985.

Coloroso, Barbara. *The Bully, The Bullied, and The Bystander: From Preschool to High School – How Parents and Teachers Can Help Break the Cycle of Violence.* New York, NY: Harper Resource. 2003.

Cook, John. *The Book of Positive Quotations.* Minneapolis, MN: Fairview Press. 1993.

Cooper, Sue Ellen. *The Red Hat Society's Laugh Lines.* New York, NY: Warner Books. 2005.

Coser, R. L. "Some Social Functions of Laughter." In J. K. Skipper and R. C. Leonard. *Social Interaction and Patient Care.* pp. 292-306. Philadelphia, PA: J. B. Lippincott. 1965.

Cousins, Norman. *Head First: The Biology of Hope.* New York, NY: Dutton. 1989.

Cousins, Norman. *Anatomy of an Illness as Perceived by the Patient: Reflections on Healing and Regeneration.* New York, NY: Norton. 1979.

Damron, Douglas. "The Preacher as Court Jester: The Intentional Use of Sermonic Humor to Persuasively Address Controversial Subjects." *Dissertation Abstracts International,* 65(09A), p. 3424. 2003.

Danielson, Marsha, Executive Director of the Greater Mankato Diversity Council. *The Free Press,* Mankato, MN, Article by Nick Hanson, "To Promote Tolerance, Let's Go to the Video: 'I Pity the Bully,'" p.A1. May 22, 2006.

Davidhizer, Ruth. "Humor—No Nurse Manager Should be Without!" *Today's OR Nurse,* 10(1), pp.18-21. 1998.

Davidhizer, Ruth and Margaret Bowen. "The Dynamics of Laughter." *Archives of Psychiatric Nursing,* 6(2), pp. 132-137. 1992.

Dean, Ruth Anne Kinsman. "Transforming the Moment: Humor and Laughter in Palliative Care." *Dissertation Abstracts International,* 65(03B), p. 1245. 2003.

Deutsch, Daniel. "Humor as a Reinforcer with Depressed and Nondepressed Subjects." *Dissertation Abstracts International,* 63(01B), p. 510. 2002.

Dillon, Kathleen, M.B. Minchoff, and K. H. Baker. "Positive Emotional States and Enhancement of the Immune System." *International Journal of Psychiatry in Medicine,* 15(1), pp.13-18. 1986.

Dossey, Larry. "Now You Are Fit to Live: Humor and Health." *Alternative Therapies,* 2(5), pp. 8-13, 98-100. 1996.

Editors of Conari Press. *Random Acts of Kindness.* Berkeley, CA: Canari Press. 1993.

Eggenberger, Sandra K. and Mary I. Huntley, "Envisioning Health Care Using a StoryTech Process with Continuing Education Participants." *The Journal of Continuing Education in Nursing,* 30(6), pp. 246-253. 1999.

Feder, Stuart. "This Scherzo Is [Not] a Joke." In James W. Barron (ed). *Humor and Psyche: Psychoanalytic Perspectives.* Hillsdale, NJ: The Analytic Press. 1999.

Feldman, Jean. "Dr. Jean," *Songs and Activities for Young Children.* http://www.drjean.org (accessed July 8, 2006).

Fry, William F. "The Biology of Humor." *Humor: International Journal of Humor Research,* 7(2), pp.111-126. 1994.

Fry, William F. "Humour, Physiology, and the Ageing Process." *Humour and Ageing.* London: Academic Press. pp. 81-98. 1992.

Fry, William. "The Physiologic Effects of Humor, Mirth, and Laughter." *Journal of the American Medical Association,* 267, pp.1857-1858. 1992.

Glanz, Barbara. *Care Packages for the Workplace: Dozens of Little Things You Can Do to Regenerate Spirit at Work.* New York, NY: McGraw-Hill. 1996.

Goldtrap, George A. Jr. "Cultural Melting Pots Can Boil Over." *Therapeutic Humor.* St. Louis, MO: The American Association for Therapeutic Humor. July/August 1994.

Goodheart, Annette. *Laughter Therapy: How to Laugh About Everything in Your Life That Isn't Really Funny.* Santa Barbara, CA: Less Stress Press. 1994.

Goodman, Joel. *Laffirmations: 1,001 Ways to Add Humor to Your Life and Work.* Deerfield Beach, FL: Health Communications. 1995.

Goodman, Joel (ed). *Laughing Matters,* 2(1). Saratoga Springs, NY: The HUMORProject. 1983.

Gruner, Charles R. *Understanding Laughter: The Workings of Wit and Humor.* Chicago, IL: Nelson-Hall. 1978.

Haga, Chuck. "Trying to Learn from a School Shooting." *Star Tribune.* Section B, pp. 1 and 5. Minneapolis, MN. October 4, 2005.

Hageseth III, Christian. *The Art and Psychology of Positive Humor.* Fort Collins, CO: Berwick. 1998.

Hageseth III, Christian. *A Laughing Place: The Art and Psychology of Positive Humor in Love and Adversity.* Fort Collins, CO: Berwick Publishing. 1988.

Hanson, Nick. "Early Impact: Schools Aim to Halt Bullying." *The Free Press.* Section B, pp. 1 and 3. Mankato, MN. January 6, 2006.

Harvey, Linda. *Humor for Healing: A Therapeutic Approach.* San Antonio, TX: Therapy Skill Builders. 1998.

Hayworth, Donald. "The Social Origin and Function of Laughter." *Psychological Review,* pp. 367-384. 1928.

Herth, Kaye A. "Humor and the Older Adult." *Applied Nursing Research,* 6(4), pp.146-153. 1993.

Herth, Kaye A. "Contributions of Humor as Perceived by the Terminally Ill." *The American Journal of Hospice Care*, pp. 36-40. January/February 1990.

Herth, Kaye A. "Laughter: A Nursing Rx." *American Journal of Nursing*, 84, pp. 991-992. 1984.

Huntley, Mary I. "Laughter and Wellness as Perceived by Older Women: Grounded Theory." *Dissertation Abstracts International*, 50(04A) p. 0921. 1988.

Huntley, Mary, Edna Thayer and Sandra Schuette. *Laughter and Wellness as Perceived by Older Women and Men: Replicated and Expanded Grounded Theory Study.* (Unpublished grounded theory research study presented to Mu Lambda Research Forum, Minnesota State University, Mankato, MN). September 2004.

Hyers, Conrad. *And God Created Laughter: The Bible as Divine Comedy.* Atlanta, GA: John Knox Press. 1987.

Hyers, Conrad. *The Comic Vision and the Christian Faith: A Celebration of Life and Laughter.* New York, NY: The Pilgrim Press. 1981.

Kaplan, Marcia and Dave. *Happiness: Lovable, Livable, Laughable Lines.* Atlanta, GA: Cheers. 1986.

Kaplan, Marcia and Dave. *Smiles: Lovable, Livable, Laughable Lines.* Atlanta, GA: Cheers. 1984.

Kindermusik International, Inc. http://www.Kindermusik.com (accessed June 2006).

Klein, Allen. *The Healing Power of Humor.* Los Angeles, CA: Tarcher. 1989.

Klein, Allen. "The Lighter Side of Death and Dying: Listening for Laughter." *The Courage to Laugh.* New York, NY: Penguin Putman, Inc. 1988.

Kohl, Marguerite and Frederica Young. *More Jokes for Children.* New York, NY: Hill and Wang. 1984.

Kohl, Marguerite and Frederica Young. *Jokes for Children.* New York, NY: Hill and Wang. 1963.

Kubie, Lawrence S. "The Destructive Potential of Humor in Psychotherapy." *American Journal of Psychiatry*, 127, pp. 861-866. 1970.

Le Vieux, Jane W. "Use of Humor in Pediatric Oncology Patients as a Coping Mechanism." *Dissertation Abstracts International*, 63(07B), p. 3496. 2002.

Manning, Kathryn. "Lighten Up! An Analysis of the Role of Humor as an Instructional Practice in the Urban and/or Culturally Diverse Middle School Classroom." *Dissertation Abstracts International*, 63(03A), p. 851. 2002.

Marr, Neil and Tim Field. *Bullycide, Death at Playtime: An Exposé of Child Suicide Caused by Bullying.* Oxfordshire, UK: The Field Foundation or Dove Canyon, CA: Success Unlimited. 2000.

Martin, Janet Letnes and Suzann Johnson Nelson. *They Glorified Mary . . . We Glorified Rice.* Hastings, MN: Caragan Press. 1995.

Martin, Rod. "Sense of Humor and Physical Health: Theoretical Issues, Recent Findings, and Future Directions." *Humor,* 17(1/2), pp. 1-19. 2004.

Martin, Rod. "Is Laughter the Best Medicine? Humor, Laughter, and Physical Health." *Current Directions in Psychological Science,* 11(6), pp. 216-220. 2002.

McGhee, Paul. *The Origin and Development of Humor.* New York, NY: J. Wiley. 1979.

Metcalf, C.W. and Roma Felible. *Lighten Up: Survival Skills for People Under Pressure.* Reading, MA: Addison Wesley Publishing Co. 1992.

Moore, Jack. *97 Ways to Make a Baby Laugh.* New York, NY: Workman Publishing. 1997.

Morreall, John, "Comic Vision and Cosmic Vision," *Therapeutic Humor.* St. Louis, MO: American Association for Therapeutic Humor. p. 3. May/June 2000.

Morreall, John. *Taking Laughter Seriously.* Albany, NY: State University of New York. 1983.

Muriel, James and Louis Savary. *The Heart of Friendship.* San Francisco, CA: Harper and Row. 1978.

Nemeth, Maria. *Joyful Spirit Newsletter,* www.joyfulspirit.com/newsletter. Spring 2000.

Nolte, Dorothy Law and Rachel Harris. *Children Learn What They Live.* New York, NY: Workman Publishing Co. 1998.

Parse, Rosemarie Rizzo. "Laughing and Health: A Study Using Parse's Research Method." *Nursing Science Quarterly,* 7(2), pp. 55-64. 1994.

Pattillo, Charlene Gayle and Joanne Itano. "Laughter Is the Best Medicine: And It's a Great Adjunct in the Treatment of Patients with Cancer." *American Journal of Nursing,* 101(Supplement), pp. 40-23. April 2001.

Paulson, Terry L. *Making Humor Work: Take Your Job Seriously and Yourself Lightly.* Los Altos, CA: Crisp Publications, Inc. 1989.

Pender, Nola J. *Health Promotion in Nursing Practice.* Stamford, CT: Appleton and Lange. 1996.

Peplau, Hildegard E. *Interpersonal Relations in Nursing.* New York, NY: G.P. Putnam's Sons. 1952.

Pope, Dianne. *The Mankato Symphony Orchestra Program Notes.* p. 22. December 11, 2005.

Provine, Robert R. *Laughter: A Scientific Investigation.* New York, NY: Penguin Books. 2000.

Provine, Robert R. "Laughter Punctuates Speech: Linguistic, Social, and Gender Contexts of Laughter." *Ethology,* 95, pp. 291-298. 1993.

Reader's Digest. *Quotable Quotes.* New York, NY: Reader's Digest Association, Inc. 1997.

Ritter, Dian, *The Spice of Life.* Norwalk, CT: C. R. Gibson Co. 1971.

Robinson, Vera M. *Humor and the Health Professions: The Therapeutic Use of Humor in Health Care.* Thorofare, NJ: Slack, Inc. 1991.

Robinson, Vera M. *Humor and the Health Professions.* Thorofare, NJ: Charles B. Slack. 1977.

Robinson, Vera M. "Humor in Nursing." *American Journal of Nursing,* 70(5), pp. 1065-1069. 1970.

Ryan, Regina Sara and John W. Travis. *Wellness: Small Changes You Can Use to Make a Big Difference.* Berkeley, CA: Ten Speed Press. 1991.

Satir, Virginia. *Peoplemaking.* Palo Alto, CA: Science and Behavior Books, Inc. 1972.

Schuette, Sandra. *Laughter and Wellness as Perceived by Older Men: Replication and Expansion of a Grounded Theory Study.* Master's Thesis: Minnesota State University, Mankato, MN. March, 2005.

Schuller, Robert H. "Inch by Inch, Anything's a Cinch." *Wall Calendar for Possibility Thinkers.* Garden Grove, CA: Hour of Power. 2006.

Sheldon, Lesley M. "An Analysis of the Concept of Humour and Its Application to One Aspect of Children's Nursing." *Journal of Advanced Nursing,* 24(6), pp. 1175-1183. 1996.

Siegel, Bernie. "Medicine, Healing, and Humor." *Humor and Health Letter,* 14(3), pp. 1-10. 1995.

Svebak, Sven. "The Effect of Mirthfulness upon Amount of Discordant Right-Left Occipital EEG Alpha." *Motivation and Emotion,* 6, pp. 133-143. 1982.

Titze, Michael and Waleed Salameh. "The Pinocchio Complex: Overcoming the Fear of Laughter." *Humor and Health Journal.* San Diego, CA: Humor and Health Institute. pp. 1-11. 1996.

Trout, Shirley K. *Light Dances: Illuminating Families with Laughter and Love.* Waverly, NE: Teachable Moments. 1997.

U. S. Department of Health and Human Services. *Healthy People 2010.*

Rockville, MD: Office of Disease Prevention and Health Promotion of USD-HHS. January 2005. http://www.healthypeople.gov (accessed July 2006).

U. S. Secret Service and Department of Education. *Threat Assessments in Schools: A Guide to Managing Threatening Situations and to Creating Safe School Climates.* U.S Secret Service and Department of Education. 2004.

Vaillant, George E. *Aging Well: Surprising Guideposts to a Happier Life from the Landmark Harvard Study of Adult Development.* Boston, MA: Little, Brown. 2002.

Wallis, Claudia. "The New Science of Happiness" *Time,* A7-A9. January 17, 2005.

Walsh, James J. *Laughter and Health.* New York, NY: D. Appleton and Company. 1928.

Weeks, Ann. *Take What You Do Seriously, But Take Yourself Lightly.* Louisville, KY: Dr. Ann E. Weeks Enterprises. http://www.HealingPassages.com (accessed July 2006).

Weil, Andrew. "Aging Naturally." *Time,* pp. 60-70. October 17, 2005.

Weil, Andrew. *Health and Healing.* Boston, MA: Houghton Mifflin Company. 1995.

Wickberg, Daniel. *The Senses of Humor: Self and Laughter in Modern America.* Ithaca, NY: Cornell University Press. 1998.

Williams, Pat. *Winning with One-Liners.* Dearfield Beach, FL: Health Communications, Inc. 2002.

Wooten, Patty. "You've Got to Be Kidding: Humor Skills for Surviving Managed Care." *Dermatology Nursing,* 9(6), pp. 423-429. 1997.

Wooten, Patty. *Heart, Humor, and Healing.* Santa Cruz, CA: Jest Press. 1994.

Yanni. "Enchantment." *In My Time* (CD). Los Angeles, CA: Private Music. 1993.

Zehnwirth, Harry, M.D. "Tickle Therapy." *Journal of Pediatrics and Child Health,* 39(9). 2003.

# References

Adams, Patch. *House Calls: How We Can All Heal the World One Visit at a Time.* San Francisco, CA: Robert D. Reed Publishers. 1998.

Ader, Robert. *Psychoneuroimmunology.* New York: Academic Press. 1991.

Anderson, Dale L. *J'Arm: For the Health of It.* Minneapolis, MN: CompCare. 1991.

Andrews, Brenda. "The Magic of Humor," *Therapeutic Humor,* 13(3), p. 6. St. Louis, MO: American Association for Therapeutic Humor. 1999.

Bennett, Mary P., Jan M Zeller, Lisa Rosenberg and Judy McCann. "The Effect of Mirthful Laughter on Stress and Natural Killer Cell Activity." *Alternative Therapies in Health and Medicine,* 9(2), 38-45. 2003.

Berger, Peter L. *Redeeming Laughter: The Comic Dimension of Human Experience.* New York, NY: Walter De Gruyter. 1997.

Bolton, Martha. *Ha! Humor for the Lighter Side of Life.* West Monroe, LA: Howard Publishing. 2006.

Bombeck, Erma. *Family: The Ties That Bind and Gag.* New York, NY: McGraw-Hill.1987.

Bosker, Gideon (ed). *Medicine Is the Best Laughter.* Chicago, IL: Mosby. 1995.

Boskin, Joseph. *Rebellious Laughter: People's Humor in American Culture.* Syracuse, NY: Syracuse University Press. 1997.

Bowtell, Diane. *Humour for Healing: A Manual.* Capital Health. 1997.

Campinha-Bacote, Josepha. "Soul Therapy: Humor and Music with African-American Clients." *Journal of Continuing Education, 10*(2), pp. 23-26. 1993.

Canfield, Jack, Mark Victor Hansen, Patty Aubery and Nancy Mitchell. *Chicken Soup for the Christian Soul.* Deerfield Beach, FL: Health Communications, Inc. 1997.

Clark, Carolyn Chambers. *The Holistic Nursing Approach to Chronic Disease.* New York, NY: Springer Publishing. 2004.

Clark, Carolyn Chambers. *Wellness Practitioner: Concepts, Research, and Strategies.* New York, NY: Springer Publishing. 1996.

Cohen, Mindy. "Caring for Ourselves Can Be Funny Business." *Holistic Nursing Practice,* 4(4), pp. 1-11. 1990.

Conklin, Robert. *Be Whole.* Eden Prairie, MN: Clifftop Publishing Co. 1997.

Conte, Yvonne Francine. *Serious Laughter: Live a Happier, Healthier, More Productive Life.* Rochester, NY: Amsterdam Berwick Publishing. 1998.

Cornett, Claudia. *Learning Through Laughter Again.* Bloomington, IN: Phi Delta Kappa Educational Foundation. 2001.

Cosby, Bill. *Cosbyology: Essays and Observations from the Doctor of Comedy.* New York, NY: Hyperion. 2001.

Dossey, Larry. "Laughter, Spirituality, and Medicine: An Interview with Larry Dossey, M.D." *Humor and Health Journal,* 6(3), pp. 33-41. 1997.

du Pré, Athena. *Humor and the Healing Arts: A Multimethod Analysis of Humor Use in Health Care.* Mahwah, NJ: Lawrence Erlbaum Associates. 1998.

Durant, John and Jonathan Miller (eds). *Laughing Matters: A Serious Look at Humor.* New York, NY: Longman Scientific and Technical. 1988.

Ferguson, Stephanie and Josepha Campinha-Bacote. "Humor in Nursing." *Journal of Psychosocial Nursing,* 27(4), pp. 29-34. 1989.

Figueroa, Ana. "Bill Chills." *AARP,* pp. 64-67, 82. January/February, 2004.

Flatow, Ira. *They All Laughed…From Light Bulbs to Lasers: The Fascinating Stories Behind the Great Inventions That Have Changed Our Lives.* New York, NY: Harper Perennial. 1993.

Friedman, Maureen M. "Gender Differences in the Health Related Quality of Life of Older Adults with Heart Failure." *Heart and Lung,* 32(5), pp. 320-327. 2003.

Fry, William F. Jr. *Sweet Madness: A Study of Humor.* Palo Alto, CA: Pacific Books. 1963.

Fulghum, Robert. *All I Really Need to Know I Learned in Kindergarten.* New York, NY: Villard Books. 1988.

Grotjahn, Martin. *Beyond Laughter.* New York, NY: The Blakiston Division, McGraw-Hill. 1957.

Groves, Dorothy Frances. "'A merry heart doeth good like a medicine...'" *Holistic Nursing Practice,* 5(4), pp. 49-56. 1991.

Hall, Laura T. "The Types of Humor Nurses Use and Their Relationship to Their Perceived Level of Stress." *Dissertation Abstracts International,* 66(04B), p. 178. 2005.

Hathaway, Nancy. "Laughter: The Cure for What Ails You." *New Woman,* pp. 77-80. 1988.

James, Diane H. "Humor: A Holistic Nursing Intervention." *Journal of Holistic Nursing,* 13(3), pp. 239-247. 1995.

Kaplan, Marcia and Dave. *Friends: Lovable, Livable, Laughable Lines.* Atlanta, GA: Cheers, 1982.

Kenefick, Colleen (ed) and Amy Y. Young. *The Best of Nursing Humor: A Collection of Articles, Essays, and Poetry Published in the Nursing Literature.* Philadelphia: Hanley and Belfus. 1993.

Kluger, Jeffrey. "The Funny Thing About Laughter." *Time,* pp. A25-A29. January 17, 2005.

Lemonick, Michael D. "The Biology of Joy." *Time,* pp. A12-A17. January 17, 2005.

Lipton, Michael A. et al. "Hope and Glory." *People,* pp. 49-53. August 11, 2003.

Long, Patricia. "Laugh and Be Well?" *Psychology Today,* pp. 28-29. October 1987.

Marek, Ellie. "Laughter, the Universal Language." *Therapeutic Humor,* 11(3), p. 4. 1997.

McMellan, Vern. *The Complete Book of Practical Proverbs and Wacky Wit.* Wheaton, IL: Tynedale House Publishers. 1996.

Megdell, Jacob I. *Relationship between Counselor-initiated Humor and Clients' Self-perceived Attraction in the Counseling Interview.* California School of Professional Psychology, San Diego, CA. University Microfilms International. PhD Dissertation. 1981.

Mitchell, Linda S. "Learning through Laughter: A Study on the Use of Humor in Interactive Classrooms." *Dissertation Abstracts International,* 66 (04A), p. 1331. 2005.

Moody, Raymond A. *Laugh After Laugh: The Healing Power of Humor.* Jacksonville, FL: Headwaters Press. 1978.

# References

"Need a Laugh?" *Reader's Digest.* Feature Articles on Humor Heals, How to Tell A Joke, and Who's Funny Now. September 2003.

Papadopoulos, George-Julius. "Johannes Brahms and Nineteenth-Century Comic Ideology." *Dissertation Abstracts International,* 64 (11A), p. 3900. 2003.

Robinson, Vera M. "Humor and Culture in Health Care." *Therapeutic Humor,* pp. 1 and 5. March/April 2000.

Saltzman, David. *The Jester Has Lost His Jingle.* Palos Verdes Estates, CA: The Jester Co. 1995.

Secrist, Mary Anne. "Humor and Spirituality." *Therapeutic Humor.* St. Louis, MO: The American Association for Therapeutic Humor. p.1. November/ December 1994.

Shaffer, Floyd. *If I Were a Clown.* Minneapolis, MN: Augsburg Publishing. 1984.

Sloane, David E. (ed.). *New Directions in American Humor.* Tuscaloosa, AL: The University of Alabama Press. 1998.

Smuts, Aaron. "Humor." *The Internet Encyclopedia of Philosophy.* http://www.iep.utm.edu/h/humor/htm (accessed May 25, 2006).

Susa, Anthony M. "Humor Type, Organizational Climate, and Outcomes: The Shortest Distance Between an Organization's Environment and the Bottom Line Is Laughter." *Dissertation Abstracts International,* 63(12B), p. 6131. 2002.

Vannoy, Steven W. *The 10 Greatest Gifts I Give My Children: Parenting from the Heart.* New York, NY: Simon and Schuster. 1994.

Vass, Susan. *Laughing Your Way to Good Health!* Atlanta, GA: HMR Publications Group, Inc. 1989.

Winer, Laurie. "Seriously Funny: The Many Faces of Lily Tomlin: Who's Lily Now?" *AARP Modern Maturity,* pp 48-49, 53-54. March/April, 2002.

Women of Faith. *Laughter and Latte.* Nashville, TN: Countryman. 2006.

# About the Authors

## Mary I. Huntley

Mary is often asked the question: "What prompted you to devote so much time to studying laughter?" In response Mary reflectively discovered that several events seemed to weave a thread of humor and laughter throughout her life: Writing a booklet of riddles and jokes while in sixth grade; admiring her father, Arden Hesla, share his mirthfulness, great story telling, and wonderful laughs; experiencing lightheartedness growing up in a family that had its own set of "hard knocks;" living a life filled with uplifting music; choosing a life partner who loves to laugh; and enjoying a family that laughs with each other.

Mary's professional academic degrees all related to nursing: Bachelor of Science degree in 1962 from Mankato State College, Mankato, Minnesota; Master of Arts degree in 1966 from the University of Iowa, Iowa City, Iowa; and a Doctor of Philosophy degree in 1988 from Texas Woman's University, Denton, Texas. Her work as a nurse educator for more than 30 years provided a variety of roles as professor, leader, collaborator, and administrator. She worked with many nurses in the Mankato region providing a program of continuing education for ten years. Edna Thayer was among the presenters offering workshops on the topic of "humor." Mary was called upon at various times to serve as interim dean/associate dean in the School of Nursing at Minnesota State University (MSU), Mankato.

In 1984 a new chapter in the journey of laughter occurred for Mary. Her daughter chose humor and laughter as the topic for a high school English paper with the title, "Laughter's Positive Force in Life." Mary began reading the resources her daughter used for the paper and new ideas about laughter surfaced. Connecting laughter with wellness became the focus. The whole notion that laughter could intentionally influence wellness for people was exciting and decidedly intriguing for formal study and investigation.

When Mary returned to graduate school in 1985 her dissertation research topic evolved. Wellness conferences were popular; Norman Cousins' book, *Anatomy of an Illness*, was still getting attention; and a whole new "band wagon" of believers in the connection had begun to sweep the country. Humor rooms, humor tapes on closed circuit television, along with clowns and laughter carts in hospitals were being advocated to help patients use the benefits of laughter during their healing time. Even though this was a fun topic to study, it was still a serious and daunting process.

Upon returning to her academic faculty position in the School of Nursing at MSU, she developed an elective course for nursing students on "Laughter and Wellness in Nursing Practice." The seminar designed course was later adapted to a totally online course. Students were surprised to learn there was so much to know about humor, mirth, and laughter. The focus of the course was to create a desire among students to intentionally incorporate laughter into their professional and personal lives. Learning together with students gave Mary an even stronger desire to share knowledge, wisdom, and hope for using laughter to help people access their mirthful spirits and embrace laughter for wellness.

In addition to co-authoring a book about the history of the School of Nursing cited in Chapter One, she has published several journal articles and book chapters in the areas of health, wellness, and educational partnerships; worked with many graduate students in the planning and implementation of their research; and served the community through a variety of roles at a local hospital, health center for underserved people, church, women's groups, and professional nursing organizations. Keeping a mirthful spirit at the forefront of all activities is a good strategy for making both employed and volunteer work fun. Partnering with Edna became a wonderful time to share chuckles while immersed in the work of writing a book. Their passion for mirthfulness and laughter has launched a new pathway in the journey of life.

The lessons of laughter and wellness are at times easier to talk about than they are to put into practice. Thus, even Mary admits to working at being intentional about nurturing a mirthful spirit and embracing laughter for wellness. Edna and Mary now wear purple and red hats as part of the Red Hat Society which has become an enjoyable part of creating mirthful retirement years.

*Laugh Often, Love Much, and Live Well.*
—Bessie Anderson Stanley

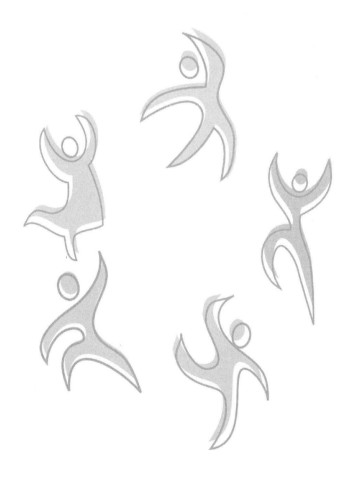

# Edna L. Thayer

Edna L. Thayer, aka (or affectionately known as) The Laughing Lady, began her interest in the serious side of humor in early 1990, when she attended a presentation on the benefits of laughter and humor by Dr. Dale Anderson entitled, "Choosing Laughter for the Health of It." She had started a new job in January as RN Administrative Supervisor for a mental health division of a Minnesota state hospital at St. Peter Regional Treatment Center, and one of 15 required topics by the State for in-service for each of the 800-plus employees was a class on stress management. The topic had already been presented in each of the typical formats over the previous years, so with the approval from the staff development department, Edna decided to prepare a class entitled, "Stress Relief through Humor." It was a huge success and the popularity of the topic spread by word of mouth with requests to present at groups such as the Lion's Club, churches, schools, and others with which the attendees were affiliated. Thus began Humor THAYER-apy, a term Edna uses to describe her "business." In fifteen years, she has given around 700 talks in six different states, varying from twenty minutes to all day workshops. Demonstrating the universality of the topic, the participants included a wide variety of people including health-care providers, educators, businesses, day-care providers, church groups, government organizations, philanthropic organizations, senior citizen groups, and clients. As part of her talks, Edna leads a laughing exercise with the audience, giving her the nickname of "The Laughing Lady." Edna credits her appreciation of humor to her 48-plus years of living with her husband, David, since August 30, 1958.

Edna is a registered nurse with over 40 years experience in the nursing field, prior to retirement in October 1996. Besides her education at Bethesda Hospital School of Nursing in St. Paul, Minnesota to receive her R.N., Edna has a B.S. degree in Nursing Education from the University of Minnesota, a master's degree in nursing from Washington University in St. Louis, Missouri, and a master's degree in counseling from Mankato State University (MSU) in Minnesota. Between 1966 and 1977, Edna was an

Associate Professor in Nursing at MSU where the main classes she taught were junior level medical-surgical nursing and senior level leadership, as well as serving as acting chair on three different occasions for over two years. It was here that she first met Mary Huntley as a colleague on the nursing faculty. Even after Edna left MSU to become the Assistant Administrator of an acute care hospital, Rice County District One Hospital in Faribault, Minnesota, for the next 12 ½ years, their paths continued to cross at nursing events, when Edna served as a mentor for nursing students from MSU, when she served on the school's advisory committee, and when they teamed to write the first 50-year history of the school of nursing at MSU.

In January 2004, Edna accepted Mary's invitation to team once more to combine Mary's extensive background with humor from doing her doctoral dissertation in 1988 and teaching classes on the topic at MSU, with Edna's 13-year background in giving talks on humor, into a book extolling the virtues of a mirthful spirit and laughter. They decided to replicate Mary's research study from 1988, to determine if the findings were similar and supportive, and then use the current study of 2004 as a basis for the book. Sandra Schuette, a nurse colleague, joined them as a research partner for this delightful adventure. This study was completed in September of 2004 and the writing of the book began in 2005. It has been a mirthful and memorable experience. It is hoped that the readers will also have a mirthful experience and become energized and motivated to intentionally seek laughter in their lives.

*A mirthful spirit and laughter are to people*
*what sunshine and water are to plants.*

—Edna Thayer

# Midwest Book Review

"Written by registered nurses and nurse educators Mary Huntley and Edna Thayer, A Mirthful Spirit, Embracing Laughter for Wellness, is a self-help guide to improving the quality of one's life through enjoying laughter, cultivating a mirthful spirit, embracing joy in the workplace, and more. A light-hearted guide extolling the physical and emotional benefits of good cheer, A Mirthful Spirit offers such useful tips as 'Use Ice Breakers and Attention Getters to serve as a great way to break the ice and grab attention at meetings and during conversations. A simple idea for a small group is to bring an assortment of caps and hats, and ask each one to put on a thinking cap. When everyone looks around at each one wearing a hat, people are perceived differently and the mood becomes lighter.' A Mirthful Spirit reflects the wisdom learned during the authors' own needs to keep spirits high in the demanding and often life-or-death profession of health care, and is enthusiastically recommended for anyone looking to inject more cheer into their personal and professional lives."

—*Midwest Book Review*
*278 Orchard Drive, Oregon, WI*
*www.midwestbookreview.com*

# Readers' Rave Reviews

*"Your book arrived yesterday, many thanks for sharing it with us!
The book is very professionally laid out, a very classy presentation.
The content is quite compelling."*

—Judy Appel, Retired Elementary Teacher, Sun City, AZ

*"After purchasing your book, I went right home to start reading it. I came
back right away as I have to have another copy for a friend."*

—Book Signing Attendee, Fairmont, MN

*"Today I had a two-hour lunch with some friends who were hurting.
I resolved to be mirthful and light-hearted in spite of their illnesses.
When I returned home, your good book was in my mail.
I read it immediately and recalled what I had just experienced at the lunch.
We had a 'fun' time, laughed a lot, and many wounds were healed....
Please get more copies of your great book to me soon!"*

—Cap Hanson, Retired Teacher, St. Paul, MN

*"I have a daughter who has some mental health and chemical dependency
problems. She saw your book on my end table and read it while I was gone.
When I returned, she was so enthusiastic and said the book was
just what she needed."*

—Retired Teacher, Northern MN

*"My husband and I both enjoyed reading the book throughout our trip to Jamaica...and needless to say became far more aware of mirth and mirthful happenings all around us. I so love a book that can cause my behavior to change...instantly! It was a most enjoyable read— and the resource list is amazing! My husband and I both have parents who are coping with cancer and other health challenges, and I believe, that a mirthful spirit can bring about wellness! We will do all that we can to encourage their continued mirthful attitudes which will make a world of difference."*

—Ginger L. Zierdt, Director, Center for School-University Partnerships, Minnesota State University, Mankato, MN

*"Just finished reading your delightful, joyful, great book, Mirthful Spirit. If only we could get half of our patients to read it and look at the mirthful, joyful side of life. I hope lots of people are getting a chance to digest the message you have shared in your book. It is so important.*

—Bill Manahan, MD, Assistant Professor Emeritus, Department of Family Medicine, University of Minnesota Medical School, Minneapolis, MN